"*Befriending Our Desires* is a thoroughly learned and readable book that offers a dynamic vision of Christian spirituality. Philip Sheldrake retrieves 'desire' as a key dimension of a fully embodied, vulnerable, and authentic spirituality. Always informed by Sheldrake's deep knowledge of the Christian tradition, the book presents carefully nuanced readings of Scriptures, mystics, poets, theologians, and theorists while remaining in touch with ordinary human struggles toward growth. Delighted to see this third edition in print!"

—Claire Wolfteich
Associate Professor of Practical Theology
and Spirituality Studies
Co-Director, Center for Practical Theology
Boston University School of Theology

"An extraordinarily beautiful and honest account of the role of desire in the spiritual life. Not a sanitized version, but a fully embodied, deeply human depiction of longing that is bound up with our humanity but also mysteriously reaches out and into something not entirely nameable or knowable—as our longings so often do."

—Douglas E. Christie
Department of Theological Studies
Loyola Marymount University

"*Befriending Our Desires* is a deeply considered and artfully written celebration of the human capacity for self-transcendence. Sheldrake plumbs the mystery of human desire in all its rich variety: its spiritual dynamism, the mature cultivation and direction of its intrinsic power, its relational implications, and its ultimate goodness. A beautiful and encouraging book."

—Wendy M. Wright, PhD
Professor of Theology
Creighton University

"The ache of the heart is the lure of God. Few writers explicate so clearly that intricate, yet intimate, interconnection. Philip Sheldrake does. He is truly a doctor of the soul, and this book is proof. Highly recommended for anyone who is searching for a more coherent grasp of their spiritual life."

—Ronald Rolheiser, OMI

Befriending Our Desires

Third Edition

Philip Sheldrake

LITURGICAL PRESS
Collegeville, Minnesota

www.litpress.org

Cover design by Monica Bokinskie. Image courtesy of Shutterstock.

1   2   3   4   5   6   7   8   9

Library of Congress Cataloging-in-Publication Data

Names: Sheldrake, Philip.
Title: Befriending our desires / Philip Sheldrake.
Description: Third edition. | Collegeville, Minnesota : Liturgical Press,
    [2016] | Includes bibliographical references.
Identifiers: LCCN 2016007167 (print) | LCCN 2016008356 (ebook)
    | ISBN 9780814647172 (pbk.) | ISBN 9780814647424 (ebook)
Subjects: LCSH: Spirituality. | Desire.
Classification: LCC BV4501 .S4367 2016 (print) | LCC BV4501 (ebook)
    | DDC 248.4—dc23
LC record available at http://lccn.loc.gov/2016007167

For Susie

Contents

Preface to the Third Edition   ix

Introduction   xi

1. A Spirituality of Desire?   1

2. Desire and God   21

3. Desire and Prayer   39

4. Desire and Sexuality   57

5. Desire and Choosing   80

6. Desire and Change   103

References   123

Preface to the Third Edition

I am very pleased that Liturgical Press is publishing this revised third edition of *Befriending Our Desires*. In particular, I am grateful to Hans Christoffersen for suggesting the project and for his helpful advice about new material.

The original book appeared in 1994 and the second edition in 2001. Apart from a range of editorial changes and stylistic improvements throughout the book, the third edition has a completely new, substantially longer, introduction. This includes helpful material on the teachings of the Buddha as well as references to the theme of desire in the striking poetry of George Herbert, the seventeenth-century English poet and priest. In chapter 5, "Desire and Choosing," I have also added some new material on the Christian tradition of discernment and of choosing well.

My intention continues to be to offer helpful insights that place "desire" at the very heart of our spiritual journey. As I suggested in my preface to the second edition, for many people the word "desire" is essentially associated with sexuality. It is certainly true that sexuality and spirituality are intimately connected, despite negative attitudes to sexual questions by religious people in the past as well as the contemporary commercialisation of "sex." However, as the book tries to underline, a spirituality of desire is much broader than sexuality. Only by attending thoughtfully to our many wants, longings, and passions can we gradually discern our truest desires. In doing so, we encounter the depths of our existence and are able to engage with the God who dwells within us and whose own longing enlivens our own.

The original book owed a great deal to various courses I taught at the Summer Institute of the University of Notre Dame as well as to classes with Anglican ordinands at Westcott House, Cambridge. Since then the book has provoked conversations and exchanges with a range of people. It also led to invitations to speak and to conduct workshops in the United Kingdom, Ireland, the United States, and Norway (sometimes with my partner Susie) in the areas of spirituality and sexuality or of discernment and choice. These experiences have helped me to develop my thinking further and therefore to improve the book.

The Scripture quotations I cite are taken from the New Jerusalem Bible and a list of other works quoted in the book appears at the end.

I wish to thank Westcott House in the Cambridge Theological Federation, where I am a senior research fellow, and Oblate School of Theology, San Antonio, Texas, where I am director of the Institute for the Study of Contemporary Spirituality. Both places offer congenial contexts in which to think and write.

Finally, I am very grateful to my partner Susie for her imaginative cover design and I dedicate this book to her with much love.

Philip Sheldrake
Westcott House, Cambridge
Oblate School of Theology, San Antonio, Texas
2016

Introduction

The heart has its reasons, which reason does not know.

—Blaise Pascal

*D*esire lies at the heart of what it is to be human. There is an energy within all of us that haunts us and can either lead us to set out on a quest for something more or can frustrate us by making us nostalgic for what we do not have. This is true of all of us. But we all know of some people who plunge into the events of life and into relationships with unusual passion. Their energy can be attractive, and yet at the same time, it is unnerving. There is a feeling of restlessness about such people. They seem to suffer from an insatiable desire for more of life—a hunger and thirst that is never satisfied. Such strong desires can get dangerously out of control. The American novelist Anne Lamott, in her bestseller *Traveling Mercies*, movingly and powerfully describes her own struggles with such passionate desire. For years her deep sense of dissatisfaction with herself and with life and a persistent restlessness drove her into a succession of relationships and to the abuse of alcohol and drugs. Somewhere deep down, however, a journey of faith was also in progress. In the end, in an unsentimental and reluctant way, Anne came not only to believe in God but also to discover in her faith a means of focussing her passionate desire into a committed love for the processes and people of everyday life.

Desire haunts us. In its deepest sense, it is a God-given dimension of human identity. As such, desire is what powers all human spirituality. Yet at the same time, spirituality in Christianity and in other faiths is concerned with how we focus our desire. At the heart of Christian spirituality is the sense that humanity is both cursed and blessed with restlessness and longing that can only ultimately be satisfied in God. It is as though our desire is infinite in extent and that it cannot settle for anything less. It pushes us through the limitations of the present moment and of our present places towards a future that is beyond our ability to conceive. This is why the greatest teachers of Christian spirituality were so concerned with this God-filled desire and with how we understand it and channel it.

In more general terms, desire is not something in our minds. Its power is sensuous and embodied. Many people, including Christians, have often found it difficult to think of desire as a key to spirituality. Part of the suspicion of desire undoubtedly has to do precisely with the fact that it threatens a rational, controlled, and protected understanding of a mature human being. Desire is not only closely associated with embodiment but also with being open to the world beyond our private selves and therefore with vulnerability, encounters with "the other," and the challenge to change. From the moment we are born, we continue to be shaped by our involvement in networks of relationships. As we grow older and progressively come to understand about how and what we choose, our own identity continues to grow from our conscious commitments to other people. To be a person means "being-in-relationship."

Sadly, however, "desire" sometimes has a dark side where it becomes focussed in destructive ways. That which is God-given, beautiful, and creative and intended to embody the depths of love may end up expressing the exact opposite. For example, the media often presents stories of perverted sexual

desire in the abuse of children and vulnerable adults and in
other forms of sexual exploitation by those with power of
various kinds, including people with social status or religious
authority. That said, our contemporary world also offers evidence that there can scarcely be a more evil desire than one
that promotes violence and the destruction of other human
beings in the name of God. I refer to religious people of various kinds who appear to suggest that God has ordered the
destruction by human agents of religious "outsiders" or of
people judged (by their fellow humans) to be irredeemable
sinners.

Yet, in terms of both the Jewish and Christian Scriptures,
to share in God's own desire for humanity demands that we
actively welcome the stranger, the "other," even the despised
outsider. In Genesis, chapter 18, the narrative of Abraham
suggests that his hospitality to three strangers is, unknown
to him, actually hospitality to God. In the gospels, Jesus is
regularly portrayed as pushing his early disciples towards
people who were outsiders and were positively disturbing.
For example, in the Gospel of Mark (chap. 6), he forces his
reluctant disciples to cross to the non-Jewish side of the Sea
of Galilee. Later (chap. 8), he feeds a multitude in non-Jewish
territory. And in the Gospel of Matthew (chap. 15), he heals
the daughter of a Canaanite (pagan) woman and commends
her faith.

In a fully Christian spiritual sense, "desire" also challeng-
ingly embraces compassion and our reconciliation with what
is strange, other, and even disturbingly alien. Not only is there
a reconciliation between God and humanity through Jesus'
death on the cross (for example, Rom 5) but also the love of
God poured out upon us as a result of divine-human reconciliation creates a new humanity in which the walls of division
between people are broken down. For those "clothed with
Christ," there is no longer Jew or Greek, slave or free, male
or female. All are one in Christ Jesus (Gal 3:28-29). Does

this only apply to the baptised "insider"? The short answer is "no," if we balance this with other texts. In 2 Corinthians (chap. 5), the universal vocation of the Christian community is clearly laid out. The community does not exist for its own sake—its God-given desire and love must be for all. Christians are to proclaim the message of reconciliation, that God is reconciling the world to God's own self. Clearly, a critical aspect of proclaiming the message of God's healing love to the world is for Christians to be living examples of God's all-embracing love and bearers in their own lives of what it means to be a new humanity (for example, Eph 2:11-22).

In the Gospel of Luke (10:25-37), the obligation in Jewish law (repeated by Jesus) both to love God and to love our neighbour "as ourselves" is presented in a deeply challenging way in the parable of the Good Samaritan. Here it is the Samaritan, member of a despised and outcast religious group, who alone shows loving compassion. Finally, in the Gospel of Matthew, embracing the stranger has a bearing on our eternal destiny in the portrayal of the final judgment. In giving hospitality to the stranger, we embrace God, and in refusing the stranger, we refuse God (25:31-46). If we truly desire God, we must also desire the "divine image"—our fellow human beings without exception. In the very direct words of William Blake, the eighteenth-century English poet, painter, and religious visionary, in the final verse of his poem "The Divine Image":

> And all must love the human form,
> In heathen, Turk or Jew;
> Where Mercy, Love, and Pity dwell
> There God is dwelling too.

Returning briefly to the dark side of desire, the need to be able to distinguish between life-giving desires and destructive desires (however superficially pleasurable) is the heart of Ignatius Loyola's teaching about discernment in his *Spiritual Exercises*. This will be explored more fully in chapter 5,

"Desire and Choosing." At this point, however, it is worth engaging briefly with Buddhism, another spiritual tradition with helpful things to say about desire and particularly the struggle with unhealthy desire.

Precisely because human desire is the fundamental motivation of all human action, Buddhism gives a great deal of attention to the difference between unhealthy craving and healthy desire. The Buddha taught that life is full of suffering and fundamental dissatisfaction. This is caused by what might be called "ignorant desire" rather than desire in general. By this he means attachments, cravings, envy, hatred, and anger. The path to being freed from suffering is to overcome this false or ignorant desire which imprisons us. Overall, the Buddha's teachings are intended to be a recipe for all "sentient beings" to become free from suffering, thus to escape the cycle of birth and rebirth and ultimately to achieve liberation and enlightenment (*nirvana*). To be liberated, we need to grasp the true nature of existence. "Impermanence" underlines that everything is contingent, and it is therefore unhelpful to become "attached." Life-as-suffering is underpinned by dissatisfaction precisely because our attachments and cravings do not give us anything ultimately satisfying. In Christian terms, this comes close to Ignatius Loyola's notion in his *Spiritual Exercises* of "disordered attachments" from which we need to be freed. We also need to embrace the notion of "no self"— that nothing and no one, including me, has an independent, freestanding "self." In other words, "I" am not the centre of existence. Interestingly, the great early Christian theologian Augustine, in his commentary on Genesis, suggested that the original human sin, portrayed by the figure of Adam, was to please oneself and to live for oneself alone. Hence, a healthy human life should be based on "the love that promotes the common good for the sake of the heavenly society."

The Buddha offered an Eight-Fold Path as the basis for the spiritual journey in the direction of seeking an end to

suffering and of reaching enlightenment. This Path is reflected in three groups of "higher trainings." First there is
Wisdom, where we learn renunciation and move towards
"right understanding" and "right intention." Second, there
is Ethical Conduct, where we cultivate "right speech" (avoid-
ing lying, gossip or slander), "right action" (not acting in a
damaging way, including killing), and "right living" where
we do not use harmful means to achieve things. Finally, there
is Concentration, where we cultivate "right effort" to purify
ourselves from destructive thoughts, "right mindfulness"
to become truly aware of reality, and "right concentration"
through disciplined spiritual practices such as meditation.

Behind this Buddhist spiritual Path is an equivalent of the
inner struggle towards spiritual freedom that is expressed in
various ways in Christian spiritual traditions. A notable example is the spirituality of the sixteenth-century wisdom figure
Ignatius Loyola, which will be mentioned at various points
throughout this book. For the present moment, however,
the themes of desire and of inner struggle, and the connections between them, are beautifully portrayed in the powerful
and complex words and imagery of the outstanding seventeenth-century poet and Anglican priest George Herbert.

In Herbert's main poetic collection, *The Temple*, he em-
phasises that humans are creatures of desire who (as Herbert
himself appears to do in his poetry) struggle to reach out to
God in response to God's own dynamic of love and desire.
In the notable prose work on the life and work of a priest,
The Country Parson, Herbert speaks of God as the one "who
giveth me my desires and performances." And in the poem
"Discipline" (verse 2) he affirms:

> For my heart's desire
> Unto Thine is bent:
>   I aspire
> To a full consent.

In terms of God, God's freedom and activity are most powerfully expressed by Herbert not in terms of judgment but rather as love. In the poem "Love (1)" God is described as "Immortal Love" and in another poem "Love (2)" God's love is imaged as "Immortal Heat" whose "flame" arouses true desires in us. Herbert's poem "Evensong" (the equivalent of Vespers in the Church of England Prayer Book) opens with the praise, "Blest be the God of love." And verse 4 concludes:

> My God, thou art all love.
> Not one poor minute scapes thy breast
> But brings a favour from above;
> And in this love, more than in bed, I rest.

God woos us sensitively. Herbert's fundamental assurance is always God's love—not God's anger. Indeed, God's loving desire is more powerful than judgmental anger could ever be:

> Then let wrath remove;
> Love will do the deed:
>   For with love
> Stony hearts will bleed.
> ("Discipline," v. 5)

The most striking of Herbert's poems in relation to our intimacy with God is called "Clasping of Hands." In it, our deep human desire is for a union between ourselves and God that somehow transcends "Thine" and "Mine."

> O be mine still! Still make me Thine!
> Or rather make no Thine and Mine!

It appears that Herbert's desire for God, as is typical with all human beings, was not straightforward. According to words apparently quoted from Herbert's letter to his friend Nicholas Ferrar accompanying his poetry prior to publication, the poems are "a picture of the many spiritual conflicts that have passed betwixt God and my soul before I could subject mine to the will of Jesus my Master: in whose service I have now found perfect freedom." Indeed, a notable thread running through the poems is a relationship with God characterised by an intense inner spiritual struggle on the part of the human heart. The human heart is a place of conflicting desire:

> A wonder tortur'd in the space
> Betwixt this world and that of grace.
> ("Affliction (4)")

There are various dimensions to Herbert's spiritual struggle. In the classical Protestant sense of sinfulness and unworthiness, there is an inability to cope with the single-pointedness of God's unconditional desire and love. To my mind, however, the struggle is more complicated. While Herbert's inner struggle is evident throughout the poetic collection, arguably the most powerful and beautiful expression is the final poem of the central section of *The Temple*, "Love (3)." Here, God (Love) welcomes the human character at the heart of the poem (no doubt Herbert himself) and invites him to join the feast. This is clearly a reference to the eschatological banquet, but it also has strong eucharistic echoes. Herbert comes across as wanting to be worthy to be there at the feast. His desire is to merit God's love. In this final poem, what is lacking at God's feast is "A guest . . . . worthy to be here." Indeed, a basic question throughout the poetic collection is how Herbert is to let go spiritually, to surrender himself and allow God to love him and to serve him freely. Basically this desire to be worthy is a subtle form of pride. On the one hand, it seems entirely appropriate to desire to be worthy. That, however, is to place our own capacities at the centre of things rather than God's own freely expressed desire. In this powerful poem, God is shown to be the one who respects human beings—nothing is forced or imposed on us, but God desires to grant us everything. In the end, Herbert surrenders his own desires, accepts God's desire for him to enter and to sit down and eat. In that realisation and surrender, Herbert finds spiritual freedom.

Just before the Second World War, Simone Weil, the French Jewish philosopher and political activist with an inclination towards Christianity and mysticism, read Herbert's poem while staying at the Abbey of Solesmes over Easter. She subsequently used it regularly for meditation, and it apparently led her to a powerful mystical experience of the loving presence of Jesus Christ.

> Love bade me welcome: yet my soul drew back
>   Guilty of dust and sin.
> But quick-ey'd Love, observing me grow slack
>   From my first entrance in,
> Drew nearer to me, sweetly questioning,
>   If I lack'd anything.
>
> A guest, I answer'd, worthy to be here:
>   Love said, you shall be he.
> I the unkind, ungrateful? Ah my dear,
>   I cannot look on thee.
> Love took my hand, and smiling did reply,
>   Who made the eyes but I?
>
> Truth Lord, but I have marr'd them: let my shame
>   Go where it doth deserve.
> And know you not, says Love, who bore the blame?
>   My dear, then I will serve.
> You must sit down says Love, and taste my meat:
>   So I did sit and eat.
> ("Love (3)")

Our desire is a rich, intense, and challenging force in our lives. While the word, from a contemporary human perspective, is closely associated with human sexuality its power and potential is much wider and deeper. Many of the greatest

Christian spiritual teachers and mystics such as Augustine, Julian of Norwich, Ignatius Loyola, or some of the seventeenth-century Anglican spiritual writers focus on the language of "desire," longing, yearning, as the fundamental key to our spiritual growth. All of these teachers, however, also note that while desire is a God-given energy that drives us onwards on the spiritual journey, our deepest desire needs to be carefully distinguished from our immediate wants or attractions. From this perception grew the Christian tradition of discernment as the basis for choosing well. All great spiritual traditions seek to identify an object of desire worthy of our human potential and that draws us beyond the superficial or the self-absorbed. The object of our deepest desire, however, which we name as God or the Absolute, is necessarily beyond what can be definitively described, possessed, or controlled. In that sense, the word "desire" expresses a movement ever onward towards an indefinable future.

In this book I seek to explore the role of desire in our quest for God, in prayer, in relation to our sexuality, as we make choices and are challenged to respond to change. In my case, I both am and am not the same person who wrote the original version of this book over twenty years ago and then first revised it more than ten years ago. My personal journey of desire since the original book has involved considerable, even painful changes as I first moved out of a religious community into family life, then changed my work patterns and lived in new places. This further modest revision is a reflection of my continuing journey.

When all is said and done, each of us is a work in progress and will continue to be so for as long as we live. And the key to it all is our desire, how we respond to it and seek to shape it.

Chapter One

A Spirituality of Desire?

> Abruptly, Florence asked, "Is there nothing that you long
>   for, quite passionately? *Want?*"
> "Oh, all human beings have aspirations!"
> "Aspirations! I was not talking of anything so elevated.
>   *Wants . . .* Desires."
> Florence looked round the garden wildly. It was cold and
> almost dark and the rain had begun again. In the buildings
> behind them, she felt the presence of studious, purposeful,
> dedicated young women.
> "This . . ." she gestured. "I could never aspire to this."
> Nor ever want it, she realised. For the air would surely
>   suffocate her.
>
> —Susan Hill, *Air and Angels*

Although those of us who have lived in Cambridge know
otherwise, the rarefied atmosphere of the University
colleges and their aspirations, so deftly captured in Susan
Hill's novel *Air and Angels*, appears to be the complete
opposite of the passion and restlessness of desire. Ancient
universities seem more at home with ideals and elevated emotions. But one of the novel's characters, Florence, has more
down to earth feelings that appear to be beyond the grasp of
her friend Thea, a university teacher, as they share afternoon
tea. For, although she cannot afford to admit it too explicitly, Florence desires Thomas Cavendish, the irreproachable

clergyman, and is seeking some way, from whatever source, to achieve her end.

A similar contrast between, on the one hand, the earthiness and concrete quality of desires, wants, longings, or passions and, on the other, more elevated ideals and emotions, has also been common in Christian thinking. In popular presentations of Christian history, it is the elevated, apparently more "spiritual" values, rather than the earthy, that have come to be associated with the dedication, purpose, and virtue of serious believers or aspiring saints. Conventional images of holiness do not encourage us to befriend our desires. Indeed, they usually suggest that saints, if they ever showed signs of having personal desires at all, soon lose them in some overwhelming conversion experience. In Hill's novel, it is true that Florence's desire is not a very healthy one but has the quality of obsession and possessiveness. Not all desire is, however, of this kind. The problem is that unless we feel free to own our desires in the first place, we will never learn how to recognise those that are more fruitful and healthy, let alone how to live out of the deepest desires of all.

Desire is intimately associated with our capacity to love truly—ourselves, other people, God, or the Absolute, and even abstract things such as ideals or causes. Love, we need to remember, is not simply a matter of immediate feelings. There are times, even in the most intense love commitments, when tangible feelings are absent. But love ultimately proves itself in its focused attention and its quality of dedication that is richer and deeper than mere duty or will power. It is perhaps what St. Augustine means by "intention" and the author of English medieval mystical text, the *Cloud of Unknowing*, by "naked intent."

Desires or Ideals?

Unfortunately, where human love has been allowed any role in traditional Christian spirituality, it had to be the spiritual, disinterested, universal love of *agape* rather than the engaged, passionate, particular love of *eros*. These have so often been treated as two distinct kinds of love. Indeed, they have been viewed in hierarchical terms as a higher love and a lower love. Only *agape* was commonly associated with God and therefore godliness even though, as we shall see, *eros* played an important role in the thinking of some significant writers such as Meister Eckhart.

I recall a letter to a church newspaper years ago concerning the writer's difficulties with the more homely and personal style of worship that had been introduced into his local parish. "After all, Jesus asked us to *love* our neighbours not to *like* them!" Some of us will recall the old-fashioned phrase, "As cold as charity." I heard a more contemporary update from an American friend who described a superficial type of generosity in terms of, "As wide as the Rio Grande and just as shallow." It is all too easy for a so-called universal, disinterested *agape* love to be simply *un*interested and well protected. A gift of everything but myself. Donation without commitment. An article in a well-respected British religious weekly noted that too many clergy appear able to relate to their parishioners only in this disengaged way. The writer rather sharply affirmed that she had no wish to be the object of someone's universal love! As I hope will become clear throughout this book, I firmly believe that the radical separation of *agape* love from *eros* love is a very unhelpful way of seeing things.

For present purposes, however, human desires have a particular association with *eros*-love, or "erotic power," and are feelings of attraction towards or aversion from objects, people, and ideas. Any desire is essentially personal, that is to say associated with the kind of people we are. It can, however, be directed towards non-personal things such as material possessions or abstract qualities such as success, justice, and perfection. The point is that desire is not some kind of impersonal power "out there" that controls us whether we like it or not. Desires are best understood as our most honest experiences of ourselves, in all our complexity and depth, as we relate to people and things around us. Desires are not the same as instincts—either human ones or those of other animals. Although desires have sometimes had a bad press, being more or less reduced to the instinctual, they in fact involve a reflective element. They are therefore, as far as we know, uniquely human qualities. In particular, we need to rescue "desire" from attempts to reduce its meaning to sexual libido and its increasingly murky associations with sexual abuse or sexual power games.

On the other hand, desires undoubtedly overlap with our needs and neediness, although it is still possible to distinguish between them. Both needs and desires can be conscious or unconscious. In fact, it is not unusual to experience a conflict between the conscious and unconscious levels of ourselves. As we reflect back on our lives we can come to understand more clearly how unconscious needs had the capacity to drive us to behave in ways that we actually disliked or which failed to express our truest self. For example, we may be driven by a deeply buried need to succeed, and to be seen to succeed, while on a conscious level we say to ourselves and to others how much we *desire* to operate differently! When we choose to talk of befriending desires rather than simply responding to needs, we are implying that desires involve a positive and active reaching out to something or someone. Such a movement goes beyond our temporary reactions to immediate circumstances and actually touches on deeper questions of our identity and our ideals.

Thus, to return to my comments on Susan Hill's novel, if we distinguish desires from aspirations, it is not because desires have nothing to do with *ideals*, for they frequently do. It is simply that desires have a more grounded quality than what we generally understand by "aspirations." Desires are more intrinsic to the reality of each person. True and realistic ideals have this same intrinsic quality. Aspirations, on the other hand, often speak rather more of *idealisation*, of something outside myself, indeed detached from my own experience and capacities, but against which I feel I should measure my life. If so, we can think of desire as openness to the fullness of *what is* rather than to *what ought to be*. Desires, then, contrast with a world of duties or of unrealistic dreams. Any ideal that attempts to overcome desire and replace it with cool reason is both inhuman and unattainable.

Whether most of us are aware of it or not, the early centuries of Christianity set the tone for so much that came afterwards and still influences us. Not least was the powerful effect of various ascetical trends inherited from pre-Christian Greek and Roman philosophy. These ascetical traditions presented the ideal human being as free from needs and desires—especially our apparently inescapable dependencies on food and sex. Because desire has a grounded quality, it is inevitably linked to our physical senses that in turn connect us to the world of time and space. In a way, all desire is sensual, that is, associated with our senses. It is interesting that we instinctively make this connection when we talk of "being sensible" about taking wise actions or making wise choices. We also speak of arriving at a more healthy way of seeing and doing as "coming to our senses."

The Power of Desire

In general, our desire is a powerful matter. Individual desires, like all feelings, vary in intensity. They can range from faint wishes to powerful passions that really drive us in particular directions and govern our thoughts and actions. Some are fleeting while others last longer and reappear repeatedly. But the main point is that there is nothing passive or limp about desire, for it gives energy and direction to our psyche.

The fourteenth-century Italian mystic Catherine of Siena recognised this positive and extraordinary power of our desires when she wrote that it makes them one of the few ways of touching God because "you have nothing infinite except your soul's love and desire" (*Dialogue*, p. 270). The German Dominican mystic of the same period, Meister Eckhart, suggested that the reason why we are not able to see God is the faintness of our desire. In the graceful language of desire that permeates Archbishop Cranmer's *Book of Common Prayer*, one of the foundation documents of the English Reformation, there is a difference between following "too much the devices and desires of our own hearts" and the "holy desires," "good counsels," and "just works" that proceed only from God's inspiration. Yet, even "holy desires"—the desires that ultimately find their rest and quietness only in God—tap into energies that are partially physical.

The sensual, indeed sexual quality (understood properly) of even holy desires, is witnessed to by the language of many of the great Christian mystics. This is something to which I shall return later. The problem is that if we are regularly taught to understand the spiritual life as mainly, if not exclusively, about *giving up* things, we will never hear the call to engage with life or particular issues in a passionate way. Attention to desire, on the other hand, is about cultivating in ourselves that capacity for passionate concern. Because desire is such a strong thing, there is always a hint of risk. Without doubt, some desires enslave us and others dissipate our energies. But desire can also generate power and physical energy and therefore also galvanise our spirituality. The fact that we frequently avoid such risks and therefore often lack a lively spirituality is closely connected with the frequent absence of a healthy and deep theology of God's Spirit in Western Christianity.

This problem goes far beyond the presence or absence of a few dramatic manifestations of "charismatic" gifts. The Spirit blowing where it wills is the risky, wild, and profligate side of God inviting us to a similar risky freedom and a willingness to pour ourselves out into situations, commitments and relationships. The Spirit is vulnerable as well as powerful. To allow ourselves actively to desire is also to be vulnerable. The Spirit of God given to us leads us not only into all truth but also into the vulnerability of Jesus' way. But to take such risks is at the same time to know ourselves to be held securely and to be safe at some deep and essential level beyond our own powers to control. The Spirit is also the indwelling power of God in the heart of each of us, sustaining us.

Should I Have Desires?

On several occasions I have been struck by two common reactions to the idea of a spirituality of desire. These sum up the human and spiritual dilemma. The first reaction is, "I have so many desires that I don't know what to do with them." Such a feeling is partly related to our fears and sense that we lack control over our inner life. But the variety of desires is also confusing. This makes our experience of desire appear ambiguous, with no reliable means of distinguishing between the superficial and the deep, the healthy and the unhealthy ones. There are certainly many conflicts that we shall have to face if we decide to take our desires seriously. Perhaps we are tempted to feel that it would be safer to treat them all with equal suspicion and to try to live (at least in our better moments) in reference to more objective values.

The second reaction goes something along these lines. "I was taught not to have desires. Or rather, I was given the message from childhood onwards that it was important to fulfil the desires of certain other important people in my life." So, even more powerful than the *oughts* and *shoulds* of objective values were the people in reference to whose desire or will we were taught to live. These might be parents, teachers, our spouse, the Church and, most powerfully of all, God. The teaching of the Christian Church has tended to place a very strong emphasis on external sources of authority in contrast to

our personal desires. Desire was felt to suggest private judgment and the uncontrollable. To follow desires seemed like
a failure in obedience to Church norms in favour of self-will.
Duty, faithfulness to the expectations of others, or self-denial
in an almost literal sense of denying one's personality and
tastes all too easily became the criteria for spiritual progress.
In the long term, this was often to the detriment of physical
and psychological health. Desire also suggests passion, yet "a
person of good judgment" was often thought to be cool and
objective. As a result, it seemed that it is not so much desire
that should guide our choices but a cultivated detachment
from any strong (and implicitly, unreliable) feelings.

In his *Spiritual Exercises*, the sixteenth-century founder
of the Society of Jesus, Ignatius Loyola, invites any person
who makes a retreat to "ask God our Lord for what I want
and desire" at the beginning of every period of prayer. So
many people find that their unconscious response is to ex-
claim, "What *I* desire? I have no desires!" Or, we say to God,
rather prematurely, "I want what *you* want!" We find ourselves
stuck—instinctively mouthing the "appropriate" feeling or
the truly spiritual aspiration! While it is true that nowadays
the language of codependency and addiction is sometimes
used too glibly in spirituality circles, there is some truth in
admitting a condition of spiritual addiction which leads us to
fulfil the desires of others (even a God created in the image
of human authority figures) in a compulsive way with a con-
sequent erosion of our own identity.

Desire and God

As a consequence, many of us have found it hard to think
of desire as a key to the spiritual journey. On the contrary, it
is experienced as a problem or at least as something difficult
to integrate with our understanding and practice of faith.
This is partly because we have inherited an image of a very

disengaged God. Consequently, we do not instinctively relate to the more biblical notion of a God who is passionately engaged with the whole of creation, whose life is a continuous movement out of self, who is God precisely as the one who out of love sends the Son into our world not to condemn it but to redeem it. As Jon Sobrino and other Latin American liberation theologians have reminded us, the cross of Christ is not just an event or an act but, in a radical way, points to the nature of God's being.

> On the cross of Jesus God himself is crucified. The Father suffers the death of the Son and takes upon himself all the pain and suffering of history. In this ultimate solidarity with humanity he reveals himself as the God of love, who opens up a hope and a future through the most negative side of history. Thus, Christian existence is nothing else but a process of participating in this same process whereby God loves the world, and hence in the very life of God. (Sobrino 1978, p. 224)

Unfortunately, a more familiar influence in the consciousness of many Christians is the image of a passionless, detached God whose perfection is to be self-contained, still, and at rest. According to this image, God's will is eternal, predetermined and extrinsic to our own hopes and feelings. If we believe ourselves to be created in the image of that kind of God, we can all too easily associate desire and passion with lack of balance, with confusion, loss of control, and dangerous subjectivity. Desire is also closely linked to sexuality, which seems to have little to do with common (arguably, traditional male) perceptions of the spiritual. Desire, then, is too often viewed with suspicion as something disturbing or misleading, even if pleasurable, rather than something to be embraced as a positive and dynamic force. As a consequence, human love for God has been treated for centuries as entirely unique and wholly disconnected from all other forms of human loving.

Despite the power of all this psychological and spiritual inheritance, I want to suggest that spirituality is in fact intimately associated with desire—our own and God's. Human longing for fulfilment in God does not need to be based on our denial of other forms of love that connect us with created reality. On the contrary, all of them are interconnected. For this reason, we can validly talk of "erotic" elements in our love of God. This does not necessarily involve us in using explicitly *sexual* imagery, although the evidence from many of the classic Christian mystics is that it often does so. But we understand the word "erotic" more broadly as that passionate, specific, and partly physical energy that lies behind other human loves and deep commitments. In that case, desire is inevitably bound up with our relationship with God. The highest form of love, drawing us into a more perfect relationship with God, includes rather than excludes the best in all our human experiences of love.

Teachers of Desire

Many of the great spiritual teachers used desire or its equivalents as the central metaphor for the human search for God or for God's search for humanity. Other writers witness to the fact that our desires are vital to spiritual growth and discernment. This book is full of such writers as Augustine, Gregory of Nyssa, medieval monks with a liking for the Song of Songs, Beguines such as Hadewijch, Bonaventure, Eckhart, Catherine of Siena, Julian of Norwich, the author of *The Cloud of Unknowing*, the great Carmelites Teresa of Avila and John of the Cross, Ignatius Loyola, the Anglicans George Herbert and Thomas Traherne, the Jewish writer Etty Hillesum, and the Buddha. All of them, in their very different ways, taught that spirituality centres on desire.

At this point, I would highlight two figures as paradigms of a journey of desire. Those are the contrasting figures of Ignatius

Loyola and Etty Hillesum. Ignatius Loyola (1491–1556) was a sixteenth-century Basque noble destined for a military and courtly career whose life unexpectedly changed in a most radical way. He will appear regularly throughout the book precisely because many people see his teachings as a paradigm of a spirituality of desire. Both his life and his teachings touch on many of our themes, particularly desire in relation to prayer, choice, and change. From the moment that a severe wound at the battle of Pamplona in 1521 ended his military career, Ignatius began a journey of desire. During his painful convalescence at the castle of Loyola, he first had to struggle to discover what his heart's desire really was. The remainder of his life, a period as a hermit at Manresa, university studies, the creation of the famous *Spiritual Exercises*, and his founding of the Jesuits, was a gradual process of learning how to focus his desire in the most powerful way. He was also concerned with how to pass on to other people the wisdom he had gained in his own life and from accompanying others on their spiritual quest. Running through Ignatius's spirituality of desire is the search for spiritual freedom, freedom from the misplaced or superficial desires that imprison us (what he called "disordered attachments"), and an ever greater ability to centre human desire on God.

Etty Hillesum is a more unconventional figure. Hers is a story of deep mystical pilgrimage in the midst of violence, war, anti-Semitism, and tragedy. Etty was born in 1914 into a scholarly, highly talented, and secular Dutch Jewish family and died in 1943 at age 29 in Auschwitz. Her story is available primarily through her diaries for the years 1941–1942 and her 1942–1943 letters from the Nazi transit camp at Westerbork. She was hardly known outside the Netherlands until recent years and, compared to Ignatius, is a spiritual maverick.

> Our desire must be like a slow and stately ship, sailing across endless oceans, never in search of safe anchorage.
> (Hillesum 1985, p. 92)

"Never in search of safe anchorage." That admirably sums up the fearless and passionate commitment of Etty's never-ending search for an inner truth (her "destiny" as she called it), for intellectual honesty, and for moral beauty. She sought to be faithful to her belief in humanity and love in the face of appalling Nazi brutality. Eventually, her restless desire led her to develop an intense religious sensibility that gives her diaries a profound and even mystical tone. Etty's spirituality was detached from institutional religion but embraced her own Jewish tradition, elements of Christianity, other philosophies, insights from psychology as well as her own idiosyncratic understanding of "the God within." Two things are particularly striking. First, Etty's passionate approach to life was thoroughly embodied in her sexuality. Second, however, she gradually discovered, beyond her tendency to become emotionally involved with men in an impulsive way, how to channel her desire into a deeper and more tranquil blend of tender commitment and personal freedom. The intensity of Etty's growing mystical awareness did not lead in the direction of detached solitude but back into active engagement with the real world, expressed finally by her volunteering to work for her fellow Jews imprisoned at Westerbork and thus inevitably to share their terrible fate.

Scripture and Desire

The basic foundation of a Christian approach to desire is, of course, the Scriptures. Both Hebrew and Christian Scriptures are full of the themes of desire, yearning, and longing. The writers of the psalms were never afraid to express deep and powerful emotions of this kind in relation to God:

> As a deer yearns
>   for running streams,
> so I yearn
>   for you, my God.

> I thirst for God,
>   the living God;
> when shall I go to see
>   the face of God?
> (Ps 42:1-2)

God, too, is a God who desires us and yearns for us:

> Yahweh is tenderness and pity, slow to anger and rich
> in faithful love. . . .
> As tenderly as a father treats his children, so Yahweh
> treats those who fear him. (Ps 103:8, 13)

The consoling prophecy of Second Isaiah to the defeated
and exiled people of Israel portrays God's desire as so great
that the people's image or name is carved into the palm of
God's hand:

> Zion was saying, "Yahweh has abandoned me, the Lord
> has forgotten me." Can a woman forget her baby at the
> breast, feel no pity for the child she has borne? Even
> if these forget, I shall not forget you. Look, I have en-
> graved you on the palms of my hands. (Isa 49:14-16)

But desire and longing are not only for God. The Gospel
of Matthew links desire to the writer's great theme of justice
in the Beatitudes: "Blessed are those who hunger and thirst
for uprightness [or justice]: they shall have their fill." The
Gospel of Mark, chapter 10, has sometimes been described
as a passage that highlights in different ways the qualities and
intensities of human desires. The rich man certainly desires
to be good and to love God (10:17-22) but he also wants
material security and familiar surroundings. The Scriptures
here do not present a crude contrast between love of God and
love of other things and people. Rather the point is that the
man's deepest desire for God, and all that this implied, was
still not free to find full expression. Even among the disciples,
the so-called sons of Zebedee (10:35-40) not only desire to

be with Jesus but also seek the status and power that they believe the kingdom of God will bring to them. To desire fully to "be with" Jesus is to allow oneself to risk sharing in who Jesus really is and thus in a process of stripping away more superficial desires. The blind beggar Bartimaeus (10:46-52) contrasts strongly with the spiritual blindness of both the rich man and the disciples. His deep, intensely focused, and active desire is not merely to be healed but, as with the previous cases, to follow Jesus. In this case, his singleness of desire brings both healing and the invitation to follow Jesus.

Authentic Desires

It is, therefore, important to realise that while all desires are real experiences, not all are equally valid expressions of our authentic selves. Certain desires spring from a more profound level within us than others. Depth of desire is not necessarily the same as intensity of feeling. For example, violence or abuse of various kinds can result in a strong and immediate desire for revenge. This is perfectly natural and understandable. Yet Christians would say that, ultimately, we need to move beyond that level of desire to a deeper, more authentic level where the power of forgiveness and reconciliation can be found. Authentic desires come from our essential selves rather than from the surface of our personalities or from our immediate reactions to situations and experiences. Such authentic desires tend to reach into the very heart of our identities. At this level, the questions "Who am I?" and "What do I want?" intimately touch each other. To return to the teachings of Ignatius Loyola, "To ask God our Lord for what I want and desire" as we focus our prayer, is an invitation to us to acknowledge our immediate sense of need. But this is only a starting point for the gradual unfolding of what it is we are most passionately and deeply engaged with. Our "Great Desire," to paraphrase Ignatius, is sometimes well hidden beneath a confusing mass of often more insistent wants, needs, and longings. To move through the various levels of desire clearly demands discernment. This is such a critical subject that I will dedicate a chapter to it later.

What all this means is that the more honestly we try to identify our authentic desires, the more we can identify who we truly are. We can think of our authentic desires as vocational in orientation. They are guides to what we are called to become, to live, and to do. If we want to begin to know who someone else is beyond the externals of their immediate life story, we need to understand their desires, which find expression in both words and actions. Of course, we all tend to show off more immediately the desires that express the more superficial aspects of ourselves. But ultimately, a pattern of what we want in and from life emerges and thus provides one of the best clues to the true self. If our desires reveal who we are, then one value of attending to them is that it helps us gradually to recognise our true self behind the masks we wear. At the same time, it helps us to become what God desires us to be as expressed in the process of our very creation. This was the level of experience that was probed in the three stories of the Gospel of Mark, chapter 10. And that is, it seems to me, one of the points of Jesus' question to the disciples of John the Baptist in the opening chapter of John's gospel: "What do you want?" (1:38). Rather, it is a question of "What do you want your life to be? Who do you really think you are?" The disciples' response is to ask Jesus "Where do you live?" On the face of it, that may seem a rather odd response. "Place," however, is not merely geographical but is also a question of a person's place in the world and in the scheme of things. The response, too, seems to be a desire to come to know their "place" and where and how they should live in relation to Jesus' "place."

The more authentic our desires, the more they touch upon our identities and also upon the reality of God at the heart of ourselves. Our most authentic desires spring ultimately from the deep wells of our being where the longing for God runs freely. This is so even if the desires are not always expressed in explicitly religious terms. As a result, our deepest desires to some degree move us beyond self-centredness to self-giving. To put it another way, these desires are not narrowly concerned with ourselves but with the growth of the kingdom of God. They reflect God's own desires, God's longing, for the world as well as for each of us in particular. In this sense, authentic desires have a social or collective dimension.

There is obviously something of a paradox here. I have said that deep desires reflect what is uniquely personal. Yet at the same time, the more deeply we go into ourselves, the more surely these desires are seen to transcend any temptation to individualism. At the level of deep desires, any distinction between what I desire and the desires God gifts me with actually begins to blur. The more profoundly we reach into ourselves, the more we experience desires that are *both* uniquely our own and also uniquely God-given. It is important to affirm at this point that these remarks are true of healthy sexual desire as well. The quality of our sexual desire is a kind of paradigm of the kind of people we are and cannot, therefore, be distinguished from other kinds of desire.

Towards a Spirituality of Desire

Given what I have said so far, my hope in the remainder of this book is to explore in a broad and accessible way a spirituality of desire in order to show that it is only by attending to desires that we may encounter our deepest self, the image of God within. It is probably already clear that I believe that the degree to which we value or devalue human desire as the key to our inner growth, as well as growth in relation to other people or the world around us, depends very much on our images of God. It is to this issue that I propose to turn my attention first. There are two key questions. First, is God a God of desire? The seventeenth-century Anglican priest and mystic Thomas Traherne had no doubts that God is a God of desire. Traherne is one of the most striking and beautiful spiritual writers on the subject of desire—ours and God's—and has become better known in recent years. "His wants put a lustre upon his enjoyments and make them infinite" (*Centuries of Meditation*, 1.44). Second, if we say that the goal of all human desire is God, does this mean that all other human desires are a distraction or, rather, that God is to be found at the heart of all true desire? I want to suggest that a thoroughly Christian answer is the second.

Following closely on the heels of a consideration of healthy or distorted images of God is the question of our explicit relationship with God, or what we call prayer. In the Christian tradition, it is not only Ignatius Loyola who considered that our desire should become focused in prayer and indeed become an important aspect of growth in prayer. Desire, or its equivalents, plays a major role in the approach to prayer taught by many spiritually enlightened people from the early Egyptian Desert Fathers and Mothers to a number of the great Western mystics. People often think of desert monasticism in terms of unattractive asceticism. While it is true that there were dubious exaggerations, a healthy asceticism was, however, actually an effective discipline to focus desire more sharply. As Abba Joseph said to Abba Lot, "You cannot be a monk unless you become like a consuming fire." And on another occasion he said to Lot, with his fingers "like ten lamps of fire," "If you will, you can become all flame" (Ward 1975, p. 103).

Some spiritual writers mention a deepening of desire in association with the gradual loss of images of God. The inability to pin God down to this or that image drives us ultimately into a kind of "darkness" or unknowing in which desire alone becomes the force that drives us onwards. It is sometimes important to remind ourselves that dryness in prayer is not the same as absence of desire—in fact the contrary is true. For Julian of Norwich, "longing" or "yearning" are key experiences not only in our forgiveness by God and conversion from sin but also in our developing relationship to God. And for the anonymous author of *The Cloud of Unknowing*, "Now you have to stand in desire all your life long" (Chapter 2). In other words, we need to stand openhanded and openhearted, not assuming that we know best or, indeed, that we know anything very much. We need also to learn how to wait and, like Mary in the story of the annunciation in the Gospel of Luke, ask continually, "How can this be?" Waiting is one of the hardest lessons for the serious seeker after God. By standing in desire we need to be ready to struggle and to allow our perspectives to change so that we are ever more open to God's action in us.

Delight, play, and pleasure are not concepts that many of us instinctively associate with holiness, the search for God, or spirituality. We may admit that the word *desire* has some kind of spiritual dimension, but its passionate sexual connotations seem to lack the sober quality needed among sound and serious seekers. Is it not the case that from Buddhist ascetics to Christian contemplatives, a culture of celibacy has predominated? This culture affects the self-understanding of even some religious people who have not opted for celibate lifestyles. So, the question of the relationship between desire, intimacy, and sexuality needs to be addressed. It is not merely a question of asking how we can be spiritual with all the distractions of family and wage earning. An even sharper question is: how can sexuality *be* spiritual experience as opposed to something that, at the very least, is spiritually confusing or, at worst, some kind of loss of innocence and of our essential energies?

Our desires imply a condition of incompleteness because they speak to us of what we are not or do not have. Desire is also, therefore, a condition of openness to possibility and to the future. Desires ground us in the present moment, but, at the same time, they point to the fact that this moment does not contain all the answers. Clearly, such ideas have a great deal to do with our experience of choice and change. Being people of desire implies a process of continually choosing. Here, once again, desire comes into its own as the condition for discerning what our choices are and then choosing from within the self rather than according to extrinsic demands. Discernment can be thought of as a journey through desires—a process whereby we move from a multitude of desires, or from surface desires, to our deepest desire, which contains all that is true and vital about ourselves.

This is a process of inclusion rather than exclusion. The movement inward is where the essential self, or "image of God" within, may be encountered. Yet this journey also involves engaging with the ambiguities of desire. Initially we are aware of many, sometimes contradictory desires. How are we to recognise the level of deepest desire that truly sums up who we *are*? For mystics such as Meister Eckhart and Julian of Norwich whatever is evil or destructive or sinful is in the end nothing, "no-thing." All that is good and has meaning is part of what we mean by deepest desire because it is part of ourselves and part of God. At the heart of all of us is a centre that is a meeting point where our deepest desires and God's desiring in us connect and are then found to coincide.

Being people of desire also means that we live consistently within a condition of constant change rather than experience occasional changes from one static situation to another. Our spiritual journeys are essentially stories of continual transition. In this way, desire becomes a metaphor for transformation.

If desire is our openness to possibility and a metaphor for change, and if we say that to be human is to desire, how do we relate these things to traditional Christian images of perfection, the vision of God, and eternal life? Surely these have a very static quality because they imply completion and our final possession of all that matters? The afterlife as a condition of "eternal rest" has been assumed to involve freedom from desire firstly because there is no need for "more" and secondly because the sexual connotations of desire are assumed to be overtaken by our union with God. In this context, Jesus' comment to the Sadducees that "at the resurrection men and women do not marry; no, they are like the angels in heaven" (Matt 22:30) has been asked to carry more meaning than it can validly bear. Of course, none of us can possibly know what "eternal life" ultimately means. But against the traditional static view I suggest that it may, like the God we encounter, have an eternally dynamic quality in which we shall remain beings of desire.

> For giving me desire,
> An eager thirst, a burning ardent fire,
> A virgin infant flame,
> A love with which into the world I came,
> An inward hidden heavenly love,
> Which in my soul did work and move,
> And ever ever me inflame,
> With restless longing heavenly avarice,
> That never could be satisfied,
> That did incessantly a Paradise
> Unknown suggest, and something undescried
> Discern, and bear me to it; be
> Thy name for ever prais'd by me.
> (Thomas Traherne 1991, "Desire")

Chapter Two

Desire and God

You must want like a God that you may be satisfied like God. Were you not made in his image. . . . His wants are as lively as his enjoyments: always present with him. For his life is perfect and he feels them both. His wants put a lustre upon his enjoyments and make them infinite.

—Traherne, *Centuries*, 1.44.

I was certainly not brought up to think of God in terms of wants or desires. In one sense, the strongly sacramental Catholicism of my childhood did suggest an intimate God— particularly one who fed us in the regular reception of Holy Communion. If I leave aside the sterner admonitions of visiting preachers during the annual parish mission, God was mainly spoken of as "loving." And yet this love was mainly to be seen in God's mercy for us repentant sinners. This mercy cast a veil over God's otherwise strong natural inclination to deal out justice! At the very best there was an ambiguity about God's closeness to us. At worst, the ritual, the hierarchy around the altar, the screens that separated us as "laity" suggested a fundamental divide between our world and God's home, our experience and God's way of being.

God's Wants

"You must want like a God." The seventeenth-century Anglican mystic Thomas Traherne offers quite a contrast. For him, our human desire *is* the image of God within us. It is God operating in us and gifting us with a holy dissatisfaction with anything transitory or less than all. Traherne seems to use "desire" and "wants" interchangeably and to understand both as our openness to infinity. "Wants are the bands and cements between God and us. Had we not wanted we could never have been obliged. Whereas now we are infinitely obliged because we want infinitely" (Traherne, *Centuries*, 1.51). God is very much a God of desire. Indeed, for Traherne, God could not be God without desire because "want is the fountain of all His fullness." For, "Had there been no need He would not have created the world, nor made us, nor manifested His wisdom nor exercised His power, nor beautified eternity, nor prepared the Joys of Heaven" (Traherne, *Centuries*, 1.42).

Unfamiliar as it may seem, Thomas Traherne is not alone in the Christian spiritual tradition in linking desire and God. The fourteenth-century Rhineland mystic Meister Eckhart is full of references to the connection between God's outpouring of love in creation and incarnation and God's eternal reality. In one of his Latin sermons, designated for the first Sunday after Trinity, Meister Eckhart speaks of God giving "himself without thinking about his loving, but as the sun shines forth." It is of God's nature to love. Therefore, we should "not thank God because he loves us—he must do so! But I thank God because he is so good that he must love" (*Latin Sermon* 6). In another sermon, Eckhart suggests: "That the soul is touched immediately by the Holy Spirit because in the love in which God loves himself he also loves me. . . . And if this love did not exist in which God loves the soul, the Holy Spirit would not exist" (*German Sermons*, 10). For Meister Eckhart, this implies that God's act of creating in love is a permanent state. In other words, God is so filled with love that God is, as it were, continually being born in the soul, the welcoming space at the heart of every person. All that is needed on our part is "humility," that is, openness to receiving the Mystery:

> If a man humbles himself, God cannot withhold his
> own goodness but must come down and flow into the
> humble man. . . . What God gives is his being, and
> his being is his goodness, and his goodness is his love.
> (*German Sermon*, 22)

For Meister Eckhart (see his *Latin Sermon*, 6), the love
with which God loves humankind *is* the same mutual love that
unites the Trinity. God's love for us is itself a sharing in the
divine life. God's love is also identified in human experience
with the Spirit. "He loves us in such a way that it is as if his
blessedness depended on it." And, finally, "He gives himself
and everything he has."

For the fourteenth-century English mystic Julian of Norwich, her favoured word for our desires and God's is "longing."

> For as truly as there is in God a quality of pity and com-
> passion, so truly is there in God a quality of thirst and
> longing: and the power of this longing in Christ enables us
> to respond to his longing, and without this no soul comes
> to heaven. And this quality of longing and thirst comes
> from God's everlasting goodness. (*Showings*, chap. 31)

Julian goes on to describe the focus of God's love: "God's
thirst is to have man, generally, drawn into him" (chap. 75).
In other words, God's fundamental desire is that we are to
become united with God and to share in God's own "bliss."
As with Eckhart, the quality of God's longing is not something accidental but is part of God's very nature from all
eternity. One might say that as God's being is eternal, and
as longing is natural to God, so God's creativity and God's
outpouring in love also exists from all eternity and for all
eternity. Perhaps, incidentally, there may be a bridge here
from the Christian mystical tradition to one of the postulates
of the new cosmology that suggests that while the universe
may be finite, it may have no beginning in time.

Incarnation and Cross

The understanding that desire in God is an eternal quality is implicitly reinforced in rather less poetic terms than in Eckhart or Julian by the sixteenth-century founder of the Jesuits, Ignatius Loyola, in his "Contemplation on the Incarnation" from the *Spiritual Exercises*. The three divine persons gaze,

> on the whole surface or circuit of the world, full of people; and . . . seeing that they were all going down into hell they decide in their eternity that the Second Person should become a human being, in order to save the human race. (*Spiritual Exercises*, no. 102)

This image of course links God's eternal love not only with the incarnation but also with the cross of Jesus. The passion of Jesus is not simply God's reaction to the fallen condition of humanity. Neither incarnation nor redemption is, strictly speaking, forced on God. Our own experience is that to long for something *is* to anguish and at times to suffer spiritual pain. Equally, there is an inherent connection between God's eternal longing and the agony of suffering for the one loved that is expressed in the cross of Jesus. At the end of the *Spiritual Exercises*, Ignatius Loyola invites us to reflect further on the eternal quality of God's desire for us in relation to divine self-giving and indwelling in all things and people.

> I will ponder with deep affection how much God our Lord has done for me, and how much he has given me of what he possesses, and consequently how he, the same Lord, desires to give me his very self, in accordance with his divine design. (*Spiritual Exercises*, no. 234)

For another sixteenth-century Spanish mystic, Teresa of Avila, the fact of Christ sharing our human experience is an incarnation of the desire of God to be with us in our weakness and vulnerability. God, in Christ, knows our neediness and that we could not begin to move towards God without the faithful presence of Christ. The Eucharist, for Teresa, is where we continue to encounter the divine desire to be unconditionally available to us.

> Seeing our need, therefore, the good Jesus has sought the admirable means whereby He has shown us the extreme love which He has for us, and in His own name and in that of His brethren He has made this petition. "Give us Lord, this day our daily bread."
>
> What a great love is that of the Son and what a great love is that of the Father. . . . Yes, for He is not like us; knowing that He was carrying out His words by loving us as He loves Himself, He went about seeking how He could carry out this commandment more perfectly, even at His own cost. (*The Way of Perfection*, chap. 33)

The notion that God desires us implies that, in some sense, God *needs* us and this is a much more difficult notion for us to grasp and accept. In one of his most direct and radical statements about the love of God, Meister Eckhart preached that,

> Know that God loves the soul so powerfully that it staggers the mind. If one were to deprive God of this so that he did not love the soul, one would deprive him of his life and being, or one would kill God if we may say such a thing. For that same love by which God loves the soul is his life, and in this same love the Holy Spirit blossoms forth; and this same love *is* the Holy Spirit. (*German Sermons*, 69)

Gospel of Luke

The parable of the Prodigal Son in the Gospel of Luke hints at something of the same idea of God. Although the three stories in chapter 15 of the gospel are usually referred to as parables of God's mercy, they might equally be understood as parables of the desire that is part of God's nature. It is the power of this desire that breaks through human barriers such as those proposed by the Pharisees and scribes (15:2). In the story of the efforts of the shepherd to retrieve one lost sheep, God joys in the "wastefulness" of love. God's desire focuses on each person particularly and equally however illogical that may seem. Then, God is compared to a woman who sweeps the house for a small coin of little worth. This reminds us that God's desire is always to include all that would otherwise be lost. Nothing is too slight, nothing too insignificant. Lost sheep, lost coin—and then, lost son.

The longest story of the chapter, the so-called Prodigal Son parable, contains many rich motifs. But for our purposes, in the context of God's desire, the initial loss of the younger son is experienced by the father as the loss of some part of himself. So it is part of the father that returns, to "complete" the father, and so he rejoices. The desire of the father is so powerful that it is in some sense the real presence of that very desire that brings the boy to his senses in the pigsty. The same power drives the father down the road to draw the son home. In contrast, the older brother cannot accept the returned sinner as brother— he can only speak of "this son of yours." The older boy takes his stand on his consistent sense of duty. The problem is that a spirituality of duty rather than desire too easily results in self-righteousness. It also lacks love. We talk easily of a God of love. The writer of the First Letter of John goes further and says that God *is* love. But love is reciprocal. That is surely the inner life of God as implied by the doctrine of the Trinity—God as a mutuality of love. God's being is to love but it is also to *be* loved. God is somehow incomplete if not loved.

Passionate or Passionless God?

These biblical allusions remind us once again that the images of God that predominate in both Hebrew and Christian

Scriptures are ones of passionate concern for creation. And yet a strong tradition grew up in early Christian theology (which continues to have influence today) that God was passionless. God's perfection is in the absence of passion. This makes it difficult for us to allow the reality of desire in God or its validity in our own spiritual quest. There have clearly been differences of approach to the question of passion and passionlessness. Sadly, the most pervasive in the longer term was the influence of late Roman Stoic philosophy. Human passions were conceived of as diseases of the soul that were intrinsically evil. Theologians such as John Climacus could suggest that God could not be the creator of the passions! The virtue of *apatheia* in human beings, and as an inherent quality of God, then became not simply "purity of heart" or freedom from biased emotions leading to a vast openness to all creation but total "passionlessness." Those in positions of leadership in the Christian community needed the same distance from the uncertainties of passion that God has. Leaders were to be in the image of a passionless God; detachment became the medium for revealing God. One classic expression of this approach to God appears in the first article of the Articles of Religion (or Thirty-Nine Articles) as they appear in the Anglican *Book of Common Prayer*: "There is but one living and true God, everlasting, without body, parts or passions."

A Vulnerable God

It seems to be that we desperately need to recover a sense of God who is not so much "power and might" as vulnerable. Jesus, the image of the unseen God,

> did not count equality with God
> something to be grasped.
> But he emptied himself,
> taking the form of a slave.
> (Phil 2:6-7)

If we accept that both the incarnation and the cross reveal the very heart of God, then we are bound to say that the nature of God is not to cling but to be self-emptying and to be non-possessive. God continually risks pouring God's self out into the cosmos. For Julian of Norwich, there is the continually repeated phrase that, "in righteousness and in mercy he [God] wishes to be known and loved, now and forever" (*Showings*, chap. 35). God desires to relate to us because it is in God's very nature to do so. In the great mystical theology of the anonymous sixth-century writer Pseudo-Dionysius, which exercised such a powerful influence on the history of Christian spirituality, God is revealed in an outpouring into the cosmos and into human hearts of being, love, and creativity. Yet, at the same time, God is beyond all attempts to describe or imagine. A spirituality that overemphasises the last part of the equation, the unknowable quality of God, runs the risk of creating an essentially *protected* God. To insist, as the Christian tradition does, that God is ultimately beyond anything we can know has to be held in creative tension with the implication of our incarnational faith that the presence of God may be found in all human experiences—not least within human desire and intimacy.

Eros in God

The privileged image of God in the Christian tradition is Trinity. In this image, God is essentially characterised in the most relational of categories, love. Equally, God-in-Trinity is dynamic rather than static because God is "being-in-relationship." It is important to express the inclusive nature of God's love and that God has no favourites, in the notion of *agape* (or universal love). But we also need to redeem the notion of *eros* in God. God also loves specifically, longingly, and in a particular way and this, essentially, is what *eros*-love implies. Pseudo-Dionysius actually defines God as *eros* or longing.

> And we may be so bold as to claim . . . that the Cause
> of all things loves all things in the superabundance of
> his goodness, that because of this goodness he makes all
> things, brings all things to perfection, holds all things
> together, returns all things. The divine longing [*eros*]
> is Good seeking good for the sake of the Good. (*The
> Divine Names*, 4.10)

For Pseudo-Dionysius, this divine longing causes God's
movement out of self in an "ecstasy" of creation. God desires
both to overflow into creation and, at the same time, to draw
all creation back into the divine life. So, ecstasy becomes reciprocal. God ecstatically moves out of self into the diversity
of creation, including human beings. At the same time, each
person is drawn out of fragmentation and dispersion into
union, into the "singleness" of life in God. The power that
describes both of these ecstasies is *eros*.

To say that there is *eros* as well as *agape* in God expresses
something important both about the love of God or human
desire for God and about the "erotic" in human relations.
As I have already hinted, we have inherited a distinction between *agape* love (disinterested or universal) and *eros* love
(passionate and particular) that makes them two different
kinds of love. A married friend, in attempting to describe the
difference between her spirituality and that of so many Roman
Catholic priests she knew, said jokingly, "The trouble with
a husband and kids is that they attach you pretty firmly to
this world." More graphically, she described sexual relations
and child-rearing as "messy, sticky, and smelly!" Is there any
room for *agape* love in all this? It seems to me that this is a
problem not merely for Roman Catholic spirituality but also
for so much of our Western spiritual heritage.

The problem is that the Christian Church tends to be uncomfortable with "the messy, sticky, and smelly" quality that
is an inherent part of every kind of human engagement. Our

commitment to "the particular," whether place or people, often struggles spiritually in a losing battle with what is presumed to be the higher value of "detachment" from all purely human loyalties. The Christian community is frequently tempted to retreat from real, down-to-earth human history into a condition of timelessness and into the myth of being perfect, self-contained, and complete. An overbalanced spirituality of detachment or separation follows from a search for *reliability*. Because it tends to look towards a future, next-worldly, completion, Christian spirituality sometimes appears to want nothing to do with what is perceived of as "unreliable." Because flesh and human intimacy are affected by decay and uncertainty, they are patently not reliable. If what is sacred belongs to eternity, then what is connected with it should be imperishable. These equations and images of a detached God, associated only with *agape* love, tend to protect not only God but also us humans from all that is impermanent.

Unity of *Agape* and *Eros*

A radical separation of *agape* love and *eros* love not only does not square with biblical images of God but also does not correspond to our human experience. It is possible to see *agape*, a more universal love, as something we always need to grow into rather than something we automatically possess. If we are honest, we inevitably experience our capacity to love initially as always specific. This can mean exclusive and limited unless our human love continually responds to a call to move beyond its closed boundaries. There are those sharp reminders to bear in mind that God has no favourites (Acts 10:34 and Rom 2:11) and that "there can be neither Jew nor Greek, there can be neither slave nor free, there can be neither male nor female—for you are all one in Christ Jesus" (Gal 3:28). Truly disinterested love is not *impersonal*—it is deeply engaged and yet free from self-seeking. We can only learn how love may become disinterested *agape* in and through the grounded quality and passionate commitment of *eros*. We simply cannot bypass the call to committed, particular love in the search for self-transcending love. *Agape* and *eros* are not two loves but two qualities in the one human love, just as they are complementary aspects of Love itself or God.

If we can recover the unity between *agape* and *eros*, we may be able to resacralise "the erotic" which has too often been reduced to a superficial titillation of the senses. The relationship between the different forms of love should not be seen as opposition or choice. In the end, *eros* just as much as *agape* (Latin: *caritas*, charity) is expressive of the same drive towards union with the One. Christianity's tendency to steer clear of the "erotic" has often set the spiritual over against human culture and experience. Spiritual passion for God has a close, positive relationship to other seemingly more ordinary forms of desire. In important respects, the latter are doorways into the former. In other words, our relationship with God is expressed, "embodied" perhaps, in and through rather than despite all our human and material commitments.

Another danger in ignoring the spiritual significance of *eros* love is that this may actually undermine rather than enhance the possibility of a mystical experience of God. Combating the antimystical tendencies of his own classical Protestant tradition, the Lutheran theologian Paul Tillich actually defines *eros* as "the mystical quality of love" in his *Systematic Theology*. Religion without *eros* will tend to be reduced to moral values and dutiful rituals. A fixed cosmic order with no dynamism in God, merely an enforced faithfulness to the unchanging laws of divinity, means that stable social and religious roles will tend to outweigh the value of the great variety within our own personal lives. "If the eros quality of love with respect to God is rejected, the consequence of this rejection is that love toward God becomes an impossible concept . . . replaced by mere obedience to God" (Tillich, 1954, p. 30).

Eros in God also makes it possible to come to know the divine in the experience of human sexuality. Indeed, human relations provide our primary image of God in everyday terms. It is not so much that God needs to be brought into human loving in order to redeem its essentially profane nature but rather that true loving, true eroticism, is always an experience "in God." God is erotic power properly understood and is the erotic power between people. God is our capacity to love revealing itself in the matrix of all human relations. For Pseudo-Dionysius, God is both what all created reality yearns for and is also the very yearning itself as experienced in different ways at different levels of creation:

> Why is it . . . that theologians sometimes refer to God
> as Yearning and Love and sometimes as the yearned-for
> and the Beloved? On the one hand he causes, produces,
> and generates what is being referred to, and, on the other
> hand, he is the thing itself. (*The Divine Names*, 4.14)

As Paul Tillich put it more directly, "In every moment of genuine love we are dwelling in God and God in us" (Tillich, 1954, p. 29).

Our desire, therefore, may be understood as a metaphor for embodying God. There is desire and an anguish of longing in us precisely because there is desire in God in whose image we are created. Clearly, the desires that are significant for following the path of the Gospel are those that, directly or indirectly, have to do with God. This does not, however, necessarily imply a direct connection with personal prayer or worship. In principle, any event or set of circumstances may become a setting that stirs our deepest longings. Christianity, founded on the belief of God's incarnation in the human person Jesus, exists to embody God. As a student in one of my courses powerfully suggested: "Our bodies are God's body language." This implies that what we do to and with our bodies, to other people's bodies, and to all the embodiments that make up created reality, we do, as it were, to God.

Desire and the Spiritual Journey

Desire is also a metaphor for the journey into God as we are reminded by a medieval liturgical prayer, preserved as the well-known Holy Communion Collect in the Anglican *Book of Common Prayer*:

> Almighty God, unto whom all hearts be open, all desires known, and from whom no secrets are hid: cleanse the thoughts of our hearts by the inspiration of thy Holy Spirit, that we may perfectly love thee, and worthily magnify thy holy name.

In the first eleven stanzas of the *Spiritual Canticle* of the sixteenth-century Spanish Carmelite John of the Cross, the human (and, we might say, cosmic) search for God is expressed in the symbol of the lover in search of the beloved.

> Why, since you wounded
> This heart, don't you heal it?
> And why, since you stole it from me,
> Do you leave it so,
> And fail to carry off what you have stolen?
>
> Extinguish these miseries,
> Since no one else can stamp them out;
> And may the vision of your beauty be my death;
> For the sickness of love
> Is not cured
> Except by your very presence and image.
> (stanzas 9 and 10)

Spiritual longing is part of our identity as humans. Such longing urges us inwards to our centre at moments when the desires of the heart get entangled with the trivial. It also seems to me that the nature of longing, yearning, and *eros* makes them more likely (as with the Spirit that blows where it will) to appear in our lives in forms that are challenging, unexpected, and even prophetic rather than purely comforting and gratifying.

Another work of John of the Cross, *The Ascent of Mount Carmel* (bk. 1, chap. 2), speaks of the journey towards union with God in terms of a "dark night." As human beings, we are people of desire. At the centre of our being is a deep longing that is painful because unsatisfied. Our loves in and for the world awaken desire and may, indeed, focus our experience of God. But if we remain only on the surface of these experiences, they cannot bring fulfilment. The "dark night" cuts off human desires for a time and in the experience of emptiness sharpens desire and an awareness that ultimate fulfilment lies in union with God. The dark night is also experienced as an absence of an immediate sense of God. There is a close relationship here to the austere descriptions of the human quest for God in a modern American writer like Annie Dillard in her *Pilgrim at Tinker Creek*. For her, desire draws people to a spiritual North Pole, the harsh and furthest edge of the mystery. It also draws us up into "the gaps." "The gaps are the clifts in the rock where you cower to see the back parts of God." Desire drives us beyond the safe and manageable to "stalk the gaps" (Dillard 1977, p. 269).

A different way of evoking the connection between desire and absence is to be found in the beautifully expressed meditation on the appearance of the risen Jesus to Mary Magdalen (John 20:11-18) in one of the *Gospel Homilies* of Gregory the Great (whom some have called the Doctor of Desire). Desire has a dynamic quality because it is concerned with constant progress:

> We should reflect on Mary's attitude and the great love
> she felt for Christ; for though the disciples had left the

tomb, she remained. She was still seeking the one she had not found, and while she sought she wept; burning with the fire of love, she longed for him who she thought had been taken away. . . . At first she sought but did not find, but when she persevered it happened that she found what she was looking for. When our desires are not satisfied, they grow stronger, and becoming stronger they take hold of their object. Holy desires likewise grow with anticipation, and if they do not grow they are not really desires. (Feast of St. Mary Magdalen, Roman Rite, July 22, Office of Readings)

The Song of Songs

To return to John of the Cross, much of his poetic language echoes that of the Song of Songs. This is not surprising, for it is the book of the Song of Songs, the Hebrew Scripture's most direct use of erotic imagery, that found special favour with a range of spiritual writers from Origen to Bernard of Clairvaux, other medieval Cistercians, the Beguines, and women mystics of all kinds. The Song of Songs is *the* scriptural text par excellence in Christian mystical writings. With these mystics, including the often complex writings of John of the Cross, a highly ascetic lifestyle and a sometimes convoluted theology was balanced by a sense of God that produced deep expressions of feeling in poetry and hymns. The mystics considered that the highly personalised language of the Song of Songs made it appropriate to use it of God's relationship not merely with God's people but also with individuals. The book's acceptance into the canon of Christian Scripture, despite some theological misgivings, legitimised the presence of *eros* in the relationship between God and the human person.

The early Church theologian Origen, for example, is quite insistent in using the word *eros* rather than the more respectable *agape* in his commentaries. And it is he who effectively originated an extraordinary genre of Christian literature. The various commentaries and sermons on the Song of Songs translate what, on the face of it, seem to be pretty human passions, poetically expressed, into quite complex allegories of the believer's mystical search for union with God the Beloved.

The Middle Ages in Western Europe particularly saw a more general flowering of the language of love and marriage in spiritual writings—and, indeed, of the quite explicit sexual vocabulary of kisses and even intercourse. This use of sexual language for the union with God was by no means confined to women, even though the imagery for God remained predominantly male. It depends very much on your point of view whether this reflects an unhealthy repression of sexual urges among celibate monastics and clergy that forced them to come out in other ways, or whether it is a perfectly acceptable process of harnessing the power of human desire towards its origin and completion in God. My sense as a historian is that the origins of this language reflect a peculiar mixture of the two.

As we shall see later, it is not at all clear in the Christian tradition that the theological acceptance of *eros* in the divine-human relationship or the use of sexual language in mystical writings did anything much to legitimise the spiritual quality of the erotic in human sexual relations. What the mystical tradition undoubtedly does is to remind us of the powerful potential of human desire in our relationship with God. This, in turn, invites us to allow that relationship to move from a more intellectual faith to connect with our deepest self. Here it can be anchored in our natural powers and will engage our emotional loyalties rather than remain on the surface of our lives and actions.

Desire and Self-Image

Although our desire recognises an absence and a lack and is therefore a dynamic movement towards what will fulfil us, its liberation in us paradoxically depends on a healthy sense of our own worth. We can only truly *desire* God, for example, if we actually believe that we are capable of growth and of movement towards a goal, towards a perfecting. The more self-aware I am, in the best sense, the more I feel the pull of this perfecting. My desire that some process of perfecting may actually exist for me increases in proportion to the sense that my life is significant. So, desire for God is rooted in self-belief, which is why attention to our all too human desires, including their ambiguities, is not irrelevant but vital!

Indeed, the matter goes deeper than this. We need to discern, as we do in our human relationships, between the mature and the immature in the way we approach God. We need to learn the *human* "language" of desire and love. It is clearly possible to confuse a kind of sugar-sweet piety for deep desire for God. But that, in religious terms, would be the equivalent of mistaking skin-deep infatuation for mature love or a cheap romantic comic strip story for Shakespeare's Romeo and Juliet. Love costs, love hurts, love engages the whole of the self. Indeed, love, as a slowly unfolding process, involves a self-giving and self-transcendence that can only happen if there is already a healthy self-possession and a secure sense that self-gift will not become self-destruction. Only from such a secure place could we pray with Julian of Norwich:

> Our good Lord revealed that it is very greatly pleasing to him that a simple soul should come naked, openly and familiarly. For this is the loving yearning of the soul through the touch of the Holy Spirit, from the understanding which I have in this revelation: God, of your goodness give me yourself, for you are enough for me, and I can ask for nothing which is less which can pay you full worship. And if I ask anything which is less, always I am in want; but only in you do I have everything. (*Showings*, chap. 5)

This brings us full circle back to God's desire and Eckhart's insight that God is free to desire and to let go of divine self-containment in creating, loving, and redeeming, because in God there is no ultimate loss of self in doing so. God's way of loving does not diminish God but reaches out to be inclusive of all true loves. The nature of God's loving desire and our love of God do not in any way contradict our other human loves. On the contrary. The divine dimension in us simply enables all our loves to be experienced in their full reality. Progress in praying, as opposed to mere improvement in prayer technique, consists in coming ever closer to that dimension in me that is open to love and which can receive from moment to moment the gift of existence in God's activity of creating. This human capacity for love is generative *at the same time* of human commitments and openness to the divine presence.

> So I was taught that love is our Lord's meaning. And I saw very certainly in this and in everything that before God made us he loved us, which love was never abated and never will be. And in this love he has done all his works, and in this love he has made all things profitable to us, and in this love our life is everlasting. In our creation we had beginning, but the love in which he created us was in him from without beginning. In this love we have our beginning, and all this shall we see in God without end. (Julian, *Showings*, chap. 86)

Chapter Three

Desire and Prayer

It is for these reasons sometimes that these tears flow and
desires come, and they are furthered by human nature
and one's temperament; but finally . . . they end in God
regardless of their nature.

> —Teresa of Avila, *The Interior Castle*,
> Fourth Mansion, chapter 1.6.

*D*uring my adolescent years, when the faith inherited
from my family background was slowly translating
itself into a personal commitment, my relationship with God
and my prayer was full of feeling. Much of it was undoubtedly
naive and some of it was superficial. But I had no doubts that
feelings had a proper place in prayer. My image of God, as far
as I can recall it, was one that enabled me to express myself
quite freely.

Then, when I left school, I entered the novitiate of the
Society of Jesus, a Roman Catholic religious order; I remained
within that environment for many years. Unfortunately, the
kind of prayer we were exposed to during my early years in
community during the 1960s was vastly different from what I
had known before I entered. Feelings were definitely suspect.
We were warned about the danger of reading contemplative
writers. This was not simply a safeguard against the dangers of
youthful extremism but also fitted in with a belief that the best

kind of prayer (unless it was devotional piety of a traditional kind) should use the mind and will rather than the heart. It is not a coincidence, it seems to me, that my overall relationship with God during that time became less relaxed, less trusting, relatively cerebral, and more distant. Eventually the spiritual climate both inside and outside the Jesuits changed radically and, with it, my own approach to spirituality; but it took years of struggle, helped by wise spiritual guidance, for the earlier damage to be repaired.

In her discussion of meditation, some of which I quote at the beginning of this chapter, Teresa of Avila makes a clear distinction between feelings or "consolations" and "spiritual delights." The first seem to be related explicitly to the human activity of prayer. The latter cannot in any sense be acquired and come in a direct way from God. The point, however, that it is important to emphasise is that for Teresa, as for other great teachers of prayer, human desires, passions, and love are not only valid but also have a central role to play. "I only wish to inform you that in order to profit by this path and ascend to the dwelling places we desire, the important thing is not to think much but to love much; and so do that which best stirs you to love" (Fourth Mansion, 1.7). Attending to our desires as we relate to God in prayer grounds us firmly in our bodies, our identities, our relationships, and the concrete world in which we find ourselves. It is through all these things that the divine Spirit offers us a union with God. "Finally . . . they end in God regardless of their nature."

True Prayer

Our human experience is a paradoxical mixture of, on the one hand, a sense of connection and harmony with other people and the world around us and, on the other, disharmony and estrangement. The good connections are made and the possible healing of any estrangements are gradually brought about through particular transformative experiences within our everyday existence. These may or may not be self-consciously "spiritual." However, this is prayer in the broadest sense. Prayer is, therefore, not just one activity among others—one that is self-consciously focused on the presence of God and our presence to God. Prayer embraces the whole rich mixture of event, action, and receiving gifts that constitutes our relationship with God in the midst of human life. For the Protestant theologian Paul Tillich, whether it was in sexual love, moments of true insight, or the appreciation of art, nature, and other people, "contemplation means going into the temple, the sphere of the holy, into the deep roots of things, into their creative ground." In human beings and in nature, "we see the mysterious power we call beauty and truth and goodness." We see God "with and through the shape of a rose and the movements of the stars and the image of a friend" (Tillich 1955, p. 30).

True prayer is a matter both of the heart and the head. It is a unity of love and knowledge and its dynamism is our desire. There is a tendency to think of knowledge only in terms of objective analysis. Paul Tillich not only sought to rescue religious "knowledge" from such a limited definition but also sought to explore a fundamental unity between it, the ecstasy of mysticism and the desire of human love. "Love includes the knowledge of the beloved. But it is not the knowledge of analysis and calculating manipulation." It is "participating knowledge which changes both the knower and the known in the very act of knowledge" (Tillich 1963, p. 137). "Participating knowledge" is a pretty good description of desire in relation to prayer. For as that great teacher of spiritual desire, Ignatius Loyola, reminds us, "What fills and satisfies the soul consists, not in knowing much [that is, in a merely intellectual sense], but in our understanding the realities profoundly and savouring them interiorly" (*Spiritual Exercises*, no. 2). Participating knowledge is what matters. Attending to desire, both our own and, through it, God's desiring in us, is the way to the kind of knowledge that can transform our lives.

As I have already suggested, desire is a metaphor for the whole process of journeying into God. In this journey we both learn how to embody God and, at the same time, the need to transcend the limitations of our images of God. Desire is, as we shall see later, also a metaphor for choosing from within myself rather than from outside myself. Prayer as relationship is a continual experience of confronting choice. In the mind of Ignatius Loyola, for example, we grow into the fullness of being human in the process of choosing. Which is why the where and the how of our choosing is so vital. Because attention to desire leads us to touch our "essential self," it enables me to discern which of our choices are most expressive of who we truly are. And in the same process, desire becomes a metaphor of transformation—of being gradually freed from all that encumbers me and stops me growing or moving onwards.

It may be that we seek to fill our emptiness with more and more pleasant experiences just as we accumulate material possessions. Yet, I would suggest that a realisation of true desire is in fact God within, gifting us with a necessary dissatisfaction with anything less than everything! And that "everything" is not the same as the accumulation of things.

> You . . . live not by your natural inclinations but by the Spirit, since the Spirit of God has made a home in you. (Rom 8:9)

> All who are guided by the Spirit of God are children of God; for what you received was not the spirit of slavery to bring you back into fear; you received the Spirit of adoption enabling us to cry out, "Abba, father." The Spirit joins with our spirit to bear witness that we are children of God. (Rom 8:14-16)

> When we do not know how to pray properly, the Spirit personally makes our petitions for us in groans that can-

not be put into words. And the God who can see into all
hearts knows what the Spirit means because the prayers
that the Spirit makes for God's holy people are always in
accordance with the mind of God. (Rom 8:26)

Desire Is Prayer

True desire is non-possessive. It is an openness to the future, to possibility, to "the other"—whether a human other
or God. This is true of sexual desire too if it is not simply
infatuation. Desire is as much about self-giving as about wish-
ing to receive. That is why desire is such a wonderful metaphor for prayer. Or perhaps desire *is* prayer if we recall that
moving phrase of Tillich, "In every moment of genuine love
we are dwelling in God and God in us." In every moment of
deep desire we are in God. To know God and to know the
depths of ourselves is ultimately the same thing. "And I saw
very certainly that we must necessarily be in longing and in
penance until the time when we are led so deeply into God
that we verily and truly know our own soul" (Julian, *Showings*,
p. 289). As non-possessive, our deep desire has no limits (for
it touches infinity) and equally does not seek to limit what it
reaches out towards.

The way of true desire is a way of attentive, contemplative
awareness of myself, of other people, and the world around—
and, in all of them, God. As such, it is not just a self-in-
dulgent journey inwards but is simultaneously a movement
outwards. Contemplative prayer and action do not oppose
each other. Rather, each is the precondition of the other. The
way of desire, therefore, also seeks the transformation of our
relationships—from a tendency to be self-serving to being
increasingly non-possessive, non-oppressive, non-hierarchical.
To allow ourselves to touch deep desire is to open ourselves
to being purged of thoughtless and self-centred wanting.
This profoundly challenges all my ways of seeking to define

others in terms of me, us, or our group. That is why truly contemplative people touch, with compassion and with pain, the heart of their own self, the edge of infinity and equally all reality around them. That is why the way of desire is also a way of conversion and transformation.

To live in the heart of true desire, and to pray from that heart, is a powerful thing. If only we could reach that point more consistently! "I tell you, therefore, everything you ask and pray for, believe that you have it already, and it will be yours" (Mark 11:24). Julian of Norwich talks of the prayer of beseeching as founded on God, even given to us by God. And in that beseeching lies a union between our will and God's. "Beseeching is a true and gracious, enduring will of the soul, united and joined to our Lord's will by the sweet, secret operation of the Holy Spirit" (*Showings*, chap. 41).

It is recorded that Mother Teresa of Calcutta said that when she first started her homes for the destitute, the sisters sometimes lacked the necessary money or other resources to carry on. Yet a period of intense prayer always seemed to produce the necessary results. We should not think that it has anything to do with the sheer quantity of prayer or even its emotional intensity. It is not simply because we want very strongly that we receive. The mystery of petitionary prayer cannot be solved so cheaply. What it does point to, however, is that the degree to which we pray in harmony with our deepest desires, in congruence with our truest self, and open to God desiring in us, governs the harmony that will exist between our asking and what is appropriately given.

In a sense, *true* desire is all. If we are truly focused—what Buddhists call single-pointed—and desire something singleheartedly out of the depths of ourselves, it can be ours. Praying for something authentically means to want it with every fibre of our being rather than partially or ambivalently. We often fall short in not deciding what we most truly want or, again, daring to admit that we want anything at all. The reason may be that we fear selfishness. But it may also be that to desire something strongly enough is always to deprive ourselves of the alternatives. To harness our energies to one profound desire is to make a decision. To decide is to choose and exclude and thus to experience a small death. Yet, the experience of many people is that if it is authentic, it will be a moment of enlightenment and expansion rather than of fundamental loss. The deep desire we hardly perceived breaks through the wants that we are able to see and around which we made a conscious choice and is immediately recognisable as the only thing we ever really wanted.

Desire and Ignatius Loyola

So, I believe that desire and contemplation are intimately connected. As the great Franciscan mystical theologian Bonaventure reminds us, "No one is in any way disposed for divine contemplation that leads to mystical ecstasy unless . . . he is a man of desires" (*The Soul's Journey into God*, Prologue, 3). One of the most striking practical exponents of desire as the way to dispose ourselves for contemplation and service was Ignatius Loyola. As we have already seen, he suggests that a vital "prelude" at the beginning of every period of prayer "is to ask God our Lord for what I want and desire" (e.g., *Spiritual Exercises*, no. 48). In the context of making the Exercises, this undoubtedly serves to highlight the main focus of each part of the retreat—its "mood," so to speak. The effect, however, is to centre the whole experience of prayer on desire in such a way that you could say that desire, understood as an increasing openness to God's possibilities for us, is the essence of our prayer whatever structure or method we adopt. This too is one aspect at least of the statement in *The Cloud of Unknowing* that "now you are to stand in desire, all your lifelong, if you are to make progress in the way of perfection" (chapter 2).

To "ask for what I desire," or "to stand in desire" is likely to be an experience of conversion and change. If desire, our longing, is to be truly liberated, we must learn to want what can actually answer our longing. We need to discover, slowly perhaps, that what we long for is "the All," the infinite, rather than simply everything as the sum total of what we can accumulate, grasp or control by our own means. When Ignatius Loyola suggests that we ask God for what we desire this may also, on one level, be a request that we come to know what it really is that we desire or need to desire. It may also be a request to be free enough to ask truly for our deepest desire although we have to admit that at this point we do not want it wholeheartedly!

It is very important to grasp that when spiritual teachers such as Ignatius Loyola talk about desire they do not mean that we should artificially seek to induce feelings within ourselves. We are not expected to ask for some "appropriate" desire or spiritual sentiment, whatever we actually feel. This would be dishonest and ultimately destructive. It is worth remembering that Ignatius Loyola suggests as another prelude to prayer "a composition made by imagining the place" (e.g., *Spiritual Exercises*, no 47). Commentators over the years have used up a great deal of ink arguing about what this means! But at the very least it involves gathering things together in order to be properly prepared for prayer. At the heart of this gathering together is the person praying—me as I am. So, it is possible to say that the process is one of "composing ourselves," or situating ourselves, in the spiritual and psychological "place" where we are. In the face of God, this "place" certainly involves the truth of the particular moment. Yet the "place" is also always provisional. Thus, if we link this to asking for what we desire, it is possible to see that prayer involves both seeking to place ourselves in a "space" before God that is honest and also seeking to be open to change. Then, to ask for what we desire may become an openness to what God desires for us and in us at this moment, in this place in which we are composed and waiting. This openness to God is inevitably only partial at any given moment. But it invites God at least to touch our centres where the deepest desires dwell in order to unlock their power and potential further.

Before passing on, three final remarks can be made about desire in the mind of Ignatius Loyola. First, desires in particular moments of prayer are not totally discrete things but relate to each other to reveal, ever more fully, the pattern of our relationship with God. So it is vital to discover the thread that links our desires together. We might say that we need to recognise the deep desire behind the desires we more easily express. This process of contemplative awareness of self takes great patience and needs moments of reflective stillness. We are influenced by so many expectations and patterns of conventional thinking and behaviour, as well as fears of change, that deciding what we truly want (or, which of the many wants is most true!) is not a simple matter.

I wonder how many of us know what pleasing ourselves really means? The trouble is that people who "please themselves" are said to be selfish or irresponsible. That immediately preempts any possibility of really discovering what truly pleases the self. And yet we are asked to love our neighbour *as ourselves*. Do we know who that "self" really is and what loving it would look like? In extreme situations, Ignatius Loyola was not beyond allowing some confused young Jesuits to be, in conventional terms, rather irresponsible for a time. He believed that if they actually had the freedom to do exactly what they felt like, rather than what was expected, they might become aware more freely of what they deeply *wanted*! Yet in practice I suspect that many of us would find it hard to take that degree of risk with ourselves, let alone with other people.

Second, our deepest desires need to be stimulated, and a powerful medium for this is our imagination. Again, when Ignatius Loyola talks about "composition of place" in prayer, the phrase he actually uses is "a composition made by seeing [or imagining] the place." In the context of the Exercises, Ignatius suggests particular desires that seem appropriate to the mood of the retreat process. As I have already suggested, these should not be understood as "oughts" or as an invitation to dishonest sentiments. An alternative perspective would be to let the suggestions act as a stimulus to our imagination regarding *possibilities* beyond the immediately obvious or even manageable. As a more general principle, it seems good to expand the desires we choose to name so that they might tap into our deeper longings and upgrade our hopes as to what God might give.

I wonder whether this understanding of Ignatius Loyola's way of proceeding throws a different light onto how some of Jesus' enigmatic sayings about prayer and faith are intended to operate? "Ask, and it will be given to you; search and you will find; knock and the door will be opened to you" (Matt 7:7). "I tell you solemnly, if your faith were the size of a mustard seed you could say to this mountain, 'Move from here to there,' and it would move; nothing would be impossible for you" (Matt 17:20). I have been particularly struck by one final saying in reference to providence: "Set your hearts on God's kingdom first, and on God's righteousness, and all these things will be given you as well" (Matt 6:33). Desire *big* things, the biggest of all that God can give, the coming of the kingdom, and you will find that the smaller needs are not rejected but always included in that gift.

Third, we can expect conflicts between apparently opposing desires to be the general rule rather than the exception. We will return to this in more detail when we consider the relationship between desires and making choices. In fact, Ignatius's wisdom was that we should be worried if there were no conflicts (*Spiritual Exercises*, no. 6). Why should this be important? First, the chances are that a complete absence of inner conflict in our lives indicates a lack of emotional engagement rather than deep peace. But, more than this, the greater our sensitivity to our authentic, deep desires, the more aware we will become of the tension between these and the temptations to inauthentic behaviour that all of us experience daily.

Desire and Julian

If we can say that for Ignatius Loyola desire *is* prayer, it is also fair to suggest that for Julian of Norwich one of the essential dimensions of prayer is "longing." Julian's main teaching on prayer lies in her Revelation 14, which runs from chapters 41 to 63 of the so-called Long Text of her *Showings* (or *Revelations of Divine Love* as they are sometimes called). For Julian, longing and beseeching are indications of God working within us.

> And our Lord . . . said: "I am the ground of your beseeching. First, it is my will that you should have it, and then I make you to wish it, and then I make you to beseech it."

> For everything which our good Lord makes us to beseech he himself has ordained for us from all eternity. So here we may see that our beseeching is not the cause of the goodness and grace which he gives us, but his own goodness. (chap. 41)

Julian's treatment of desire, or longing, in relationship to prayer is more comprehensive, basic, and dynamic than many other spiritual writers. Her own understanding of desire seems to have expanded in the course of her experiences, and so she shares with us her perceptions of what and how we are to desire in order to become one with God. For Julian, our deepest natural desire is to have nothing less than God.

> For this is the loving yearning of the soul through the touch of the Holy Spirit, from the understanding which I have in this revelation: God, of your goodness give me

> yourself, for you are enough for me, and I can ask for
> nothing which is less which can pay you full worship.
> And if I ask anything which is less, always I am in want;
> but only in you do I have everything. (chap. 5)

This desire is so great that we would not be content without
God even if we had all other things.

> The natural desire of our soul is so great and so immea-
> surable that if all the nobility which God ever created in
> heaven and on earth were given to us for our joy and
> our comfort, if we did not see his own fair blessed face,
> still we should never cease to mourn and to weep in the
> spirit. (chap. 72)

"For [God] wants us to know that in a short time we shall see
clearly in him all that we desire." For Julian, it was not knowledge but desire itself, and its strength, that really counted.
"Still it seemed to me humble and petty in comparison with
the great desire which the soul has to see God" (chap. 47).

The unlocking of our desire in prayer creates a dynamic
whereby the least encounter with God stirs us to seek for
more. The more we experience the reality of God, the more
we desire God.

> When we by his special grace behold him plainly, seeing
> no other, we then necessarily follow him, and he draws
> us to him by love. For I saw and felt that his wonderful
> and total goodness fulfils all our powers; and with that
> I saw that his continual working in every kind of thing
> is done so divinely, so wisely and so powerfully that
> it surpasses all our imagining and everything we can
> understand or think. And then we can do no more than
> contemplate him and rejoice, with a great and compel-
> ling desire to be wholly united into him, and attend
> to his motion and rejoice in his love and delight in his
> goodness. (chap. 43)

But this dynamic has a perpetual quality of incompleteness for we never come to *possess* God finally. "So I saw him and sought him, and I had him and lacked him" (chap. 10). Desire is, therefore, a permanent part of our lives—the condition of openness to God's reality as it unfolds infinitely and eternally.

Desire and Hadewijch

The fact that our deepest desire is never definitively satisfied is also a painful matter. Julian's "I had him and I lacked him" has a very poignant feel to it, as does the love-mysticism of the thirteenth-century Flemish beguine, Hadewijch, who in her visions experienced Christ speaking to her of "painful desire" and the "privation of what you desire above all . . . this reaching out to me who am unreachable" (*The Complete Works*, p. 283). Hadewijch has a great deal more to say about the unquiet nature of desire in one of her poems in couplets (number 10), "Not Feeling but Love." In our "childish" love, we sometimes want to be satisfied with "many particular things" because we mistake the "delight" of good feelings for true "desire." In Hadewijch's experience, this would be to settle for substantially less than we are called to.

> Not for feeling's sake must we learn to serve,
> But only to love with love in Love.

The difference between delight and desire offers an interesting comparison with what Ignatius Loyola teaches about spiritual "consolation" in his Rules for the Discernment of Spirits (*Spiritual Exercises*, nos. 313–336). Consolation should not be mistaken for pleasurable or good feelings—although these may be part of the experience at times. Consolation is an experience of being drawn towards what is life-giving, towards inner freedom, towards real love, ultimately towards God. It is fairly obvious from our common experience that all these things may actually be quite painful and certainly challenging. Ignatius recognises this feature clearly. And yet there is an underlying sense of rightness, peace, and harmony that actually enables us to move on even in the midst of surface difficulties. This is "a peace that the world cannot give" (John 14:27). Although, on the face of it, his dry prose lacks the evocative qualities of a Hadewijch, Ignatius tries to express a paradoxical quality in "consolation'" similar to that present in her more poetic descriptions of desire.

For Hadewijch, in order to reach the unreachable God who is Love, we need to love without rest and "desire above measure"—that is, beyond reason and thought. So our spirit, even

> when it feels misery,
> It can learn to know Love's mode of action.
> The effect of divine Love in us is that,
>
> > The proximity of the nature of Love
> > Deprives the soul of its rest:
> > The more Love comes, the more she steals.

To those who really seek to live, riskily, in Love and who enter what Hadewijch calls the divine "abyss," Love "gives an unquiet life." Why? Because divine Love "causes hearts, in Love, to be in constant striving."

> Desires of love, moreover, cannot
> By all these explanations be quieted.
> Desire strives in all things for more than it possesses:
> Love does not allow it to have any rest.

In a daring and controversial statement (also present in her Letter 8 and Vision 13), Hadewijch suggests that a "noble unfaith" is higher than "fidelity." While "fidelity" is related to reason and "often lets desire be satisfied," unfaith "never allows desire any rest in any fidelity." This "unfaith," which is expressed as a negative quality, is difficult to define but is perhaps also best understood if approached negatively! It consists of living in the absence of consoling feelings. It is the opposite of peaceful rest that settles for less than the All. It turns our spirit away from taking pleasure "in what it has in hand." It is suspicious even of divine Love in the sense of anything that can be grasped. Thus, even at the heart of Hadewijch's rich spirituality of love, the total otherness of God is somehow expressed.

There appear to be similarities here to the more austere mysticism of "unknowing" present, for example, in Meister Eckhart's paradoxical teaching that Christians should be so poor that they do not even have God, or in the writings of the important twentieth-century Welsh priest-poet R. S. Thomas:

> Why no! I never thought other than
> That God is that great absence
> In our lives, the empty silence
> Within, the place where we go
> Seeking, not in hope to
> Arrive or find.
> (Thomas 1984, "Via Negativa")

The moment you feel yourself to be in definitive contact with the reality of God, you have missed God. Hadewijch's unfaith bypasses what is manageable and controllable in human terms. There is a painful quality to all true love because love is ultimately there for the sake of love—not for feelings of security or satisfaction. If we have ever found ourselves continuing to love "beyond the immediate facts" in our relationship with another person, we will have a small inkling of what Hadewijch understands about our relationship with God.

Active Desire

If desire in prayer is unlocked, there is another dynamic present that consists of a gradual movement not only towards our own deepest desire but also, in and through that, towards God's own desiring within us. As Julian suggests,

> For the whole reason why we pray is to be united into the vision and contemplation of him to whom we pray, wonderfully rejoicing with reverent fear, and with so much sweetness and delight in him that we cannot pray at all except as he moves us at the time.
>
> And so I saw that when we see the need for us to pray, then our Lord God is following us, helping our desire. (*Showings*, chap. 43)

In other words, God is the one who places desire in our hearts and who is the completion of all true desires. "I am he who makes you to long; I am he, the endless fulfilling of all true desires" (*Showings*, chap. 59). It is not that to desire God is the only valid desire, with other, more physical or material desires being mere distractions. It is not a matter of choosing between God and other loves or needs. Julian was quite explicit that she wrote about her mystical experiences for the benefit of all her fellow Christians, whatever their lifestyle. Although she had chosen a solitary life at some point in her adulthood, she clearly did not believe that it was the only life compatible with contemplative mysticism. It would therefore be better to say that Julian taught that if our desires, whatever they are, are true to our deepest self, they are God-filled.

For Julian, as for many mystics, desire is not entirely passive—some kind of lingering longing. It is active and it is powerful. Even in the more passive, mystical Sixth Mansion of her *Interior Castle*, Teresa of Avila writes of the soul being brought to desire God "vehemently." And throughout *The Cloud of Unknowing*, the author links desire, or its equivalents, to such active verbs as "labour": "You are to smite upon that thick cloud of unknowing with a sharp dart of longing love" (chap. 6). Desire often involves what we might call an "intentional longing," or focused longing, for God. That seems to be an especially good description of what Ignatius Loyola implies when he suggests that we *ask* for what we desire. But it is also part of the teaching on contemplation in *The Cloud of Unknowing*. There, the language of stripping ourselves of every thought and desire for what is not God does not imply the *destruction* of human desire but its intense concentration that can fan a spark into a flame. For, if directed towards many objects separately, our desire is dissipated. The aim of contemplation is to unite all our desires towards one object in a concentrated intensity.

Is our state of desire, our focused longing, a permanent condition? Surely, once we are united with God our desire is fulfilled. Well, in one sense we are from the start united with God who is unchangeable goodness. This is the precondition of our journeying, not merely the final conclusion. "For our soul is so wholly united to God, through his own goodness, that between God and our soul nothing can interpose" (*Showings*, chap. 46). Yet, it is this very union with God that deepens desire. Material needs may be satisfied, but that is never so of the desire for the infinite. Rather, the paradox is that as God's presence is perceived more deeply, so desire is increased rather than satisfied. For Julian, the reality of God is as a God of desire, and this quality in God lasts until the end of time.

> Which desire, longing and thirst, as I see it, were in him from without beginning; and he will have this until the time that the last soul which will be saved has come up into his bliss. (chap. 31)

Whether we can understand desire as existing even beyond this, in whatever we mean by "eternal life," is something to which I will return later.

So, it would appear that longing and desire, ours and God's, are qualities that remain until we are caught into God's "bliss." We never possess God or encompass the infinite. For us, in relation to God, there will always be the promise of more, because we cannot experience any limit to what it is we ultimately desire. As one of the great spiritual teachers of the Eastern Church, Gregory of Nyssa, reminds us, communion with God is an experience of continual expansion. In meeting God, we can never be filled in an ultimate sense. Desire, therefore, as openness to possibility and to love ever remains in us. "This truly is the vision of God: never to be satisfied in the desire to see him. But one must always, by looking at what he can see, rekindle his desire to see more" (Gregory of Nyssa, *The Life of Moses*, bk. 2, 239).

Chapter Four

Desire and Sexuality

Where, like a pillow on a bed,
A Pregnant banke swel'd up, to rest
The violets reclining head,
Sat we two, one anothers best.
Our hands were firmely cimented
With a fast balme, which thence did spring,
Our eye-beames twisted, and did thred
Our eyes, upon one double string. . . .

This Extasie doth unperplex
(We said) and tell us what we love,
Wee see by this, it was not sexe,
Wee see, we saw not what did move:
But as all severall soules containe
Mixture of things, they know not what,
Love, these mixt soules doth mixe againe,
And makes both one, each this and that. . . .

But O alas, so long, so farre
Our bodies why doe wee forbeare?
They'are ours, though they'are not wee, Wee are
The intelligences, they the spheare.
We owe them thankes, because they thus,
Did us, to us, at first convey,
Yeelded their forces, sense, to us,
Nor are drosse to us, but allay.

On man heavens influence workes not so,
But that it first imprints the ayre,
Soe soule into the soule may flow,
Though it to body first repaire. . . .

To'our bodies turne wee then, that so
Weake men on love reveal'd may looke;
Loves mysteries in soules doe grow,
But yet the body is his booke. . . .

—John Donne, "The Extasie"

*M*any years ago I was accompanying an older married man during his retreat. In his prayer, he had been focusing on the familiar image of the potter in the opening verses of the book of Jeremiah, chapter 18. "Yes, like clay in the potter's hand, so are you in mine, House of Israel." As he identified himself with the clay, the man found to his surprise that the thought of God's hands shaping him, especially re-forming him, was very frightening. We agreed together that he should return to the same Scripture passage in the course of the next day's prayer to see whether there would be any further enlightenment. Although it was unplanned and not his usual form of prayer, the man found himself visualising in his imagination the hands of God reaching out towards him. He tried honestly to invite God to shape him. But he could not do so, for the experience still felt too threatening. As he described it to me during our conversation the next day, he eventually gave up the struggle and simply sat blankly with himself, his fears, and God. Quite unexpectedly, the image returned of hands reaching out towards him. Before he could once again recoil in fear, however, he saw that God's hands were the hands of his wife that had caressed him so many times during their long marriage. It was a profound conversion experience on several levels.

Clearly, something important about the man's fearful images of God was made explicit and healed in a substantial way. The man also took a step forward in the process of lowering his instinctive defences and letting go in trust. Most striking of all in that experience, however, the man understood that God's touch had been at the heart of all his human love and sexual intimacy.

The Christian mystical tradition has often used the language of sexual love and eroticism both in terms of God's way of relating to humankind and our way of union with God. This, however, has usually implied the *transformation* of the sexual energy of "*eros*" into distinctively spiritual channels. The trouble is that, from quite an early stage of its history, Christianity has all too often treated sexuality and "the erotic" as particularly symptomatic of a world that was fallen away from God. So sexual ecstasy was not to be compared with spiritual ecstasy and, consequently, was unable to contribute to our relationship with God. Usually, sexual feelings were considered a profound problem! At an ecumenical workshop on human sexuality in which I was involved, a number of people commented that some members of their churches still thought of sex as a necessary evil and not as a gift of God to be enjoyed. For classical Christianity, it was human sexual *language* that was useable in terms of human encounters with God—not human sexual *experience*. The result was an uncomfortable paradox. While *eros* transformed into spiritual energy might be fine, there had to be, at the same time, a complete separation between holiness and sexuality.

Every human person is unavoidably a sexual being. This emphatically includes those in various forms of singleness, not least those who have chosen celibacy. We can try to ignore sexuality and to repress it, or we can seek to live positively and healthily within it. What is not open to us is to bypass it or to escape completely from it.

The historical origins of Christianity's traditional problems with the body, passion, and sexuality are complex. Perhaps the most elegantly written, comprehensive, and balanced account in English is Peter Brown's book *The Body and Society*, which charts the rise of sexual renunciation in early Christianity. Many factors played their part. There was, first of all, a certain inheritance from Stoic philosophy. Here, spiritual significance was accorded to the repudiation of pleasure and to the avoidance of uncontrolled passion. Then there were late imperial Roman attitudes to masculinity as the measure of what it was to be human. This involved the need to maintain male "integrity" by means of detachment, self-sufficiency, autonomy, and the avoidance of softness. These cultural values were reinforced by the theological link that was gradually forged between the wholeness, involving resurrection of the body, that was our presumed destiny in heaven and the desire to anticipate this through the bodily intactness of virginity in the here and now.

The result was that, for much of the Christian era, the perceived precondition of a profound spirituality has been the absence of active sexuality. If this was not precisely perpetual virginity, then widowhood or some kind of voluntary sexual abstinence would do. For example, the medieval English mystic, Margery Kempe, was a married woman who was reassured in visions that God also loved married people! Yet once she had experienced her first vision of heavenly bliss, she wrote that she had no further sexual desire for her husband and even came to think of sexual relations as abominable. She eventually persuaded her husband to join with her in a mutual vow of chastity (*The Book of Margery Kempe*, bk. 1, chaps. 3–10). True, in Margery's historical context of extremely unequal relations between the sexes, celibacy could be a form of social, sexual, and spiritual liberation for her and other medieval women mystics. But the issue is obviously more complex because Margery, for example, was prepared to testify that sexual relations with her husband had in fact once been "a great delight" to both of them.

Obviously, we cannot entirely bypass these difficulties that we have inherited about linking spirituality and sexuality. I want to concentrate here, however, on exploring positive ways of reenvisioning human sexuality, including its active expression, as a path to holiness and to God. This chapter began with selected quotations from the poem "The Extasie" by the great early seventeenth-century poet John Donne. Most commentators traditionally distinguish between his "divine" poems and his "secular" ones. The latter are frequently concerned with human love and are sometimes charged with sexual imagery. Yet Donne the human lover was also Dean Donne of St Paul's Cathedral, London, an Anglican priest with strong Roman Catholic family roots.

For Donne there was no radical gulf fixed between grace and nature, between the spiritual and the bodily. His vision of the human person, most famously expressed in his poetic line, "No man is an island, apart from the main," is one of connection rather than autonomy. The whole of the natural world is graced and consequently so is sexual experience. John Donne almost certainly drew on his Catholic roots, not least the spirituality of the mystics and of his contemporary, St Francis de Sales, as well as on his own experience of love and marriage, to bring out the sacred (and, on occasion, mystical) quality of sexual love. It seems that his was one of the earliest explicit attempts in mainstream Western Christianity to appreciate sexual love as, at least potentially, spiritual experience.

Even if the greater part of the Western mystical tradition has tended not to consider direct sexual experience respectable in terms of our encounter with God, it remains a fact that writers such as Teresa of Avila at least found in sexual ecstasy the most adequate analogy to spiritual ecstasy. This leaves us with something that we can build upon. I suggest that the special quality that mystics found in the language of human sexuality implicitly affirms that human loving is an embodiment (literally and metaphorically) of the love of God.

In trying to sketch out the beginnings of a spirituality of sexual desire, I want to focus briefly on five themes. First, although we opened up the question of *eros* and the "erotic" in chapter 1, we need to look at some further aspects of what we understand by them. Second, we can assert that a conscious and healthy sexuality is not necessarily genitally active. There is no really well-developed spirituality of singleness in terms of sexuality. If spirituality in the churches has been explicitly linked to sexuality at all, it has been limited to heterosexual relationships, conventional marriage, and the birth of children. Indeed, as someone once pointed out to me, the most commonly used rituals provided by all mainline churches are baptism, marriage, and funerals. The first two inevitably involve partnerships and only the latter includes single people! Therefore, it is important to look at the question of human intimacy in the broadest sense. A great deal of what may be said about sexual union may also be said of non-genital intimacy, although the sexual union of two deeply committed people certainly focuses and enables certain spiritual experiences in a particularly powerful way. Whether we live sexually active lives or not, a balance between solitude and intimacy is an important psychological and spiritual need for all of us. Third, turning explicitly to active sexual relations, we will consider the experience of sexual union as a form of liberation from the tyranny of private will. Fourth, we will look again at possible connections between sexual ecstasy and union with God. Finally, we will reflect on the difference between abusive or invasive relationships and the respectful crossing of personal boundaries that is involved in healthy sexual intimacy.

The Erotic

In the light of the kind of sexual reductionism that is so often present in Western cultures these days, it is a pity that Christians have not found a way to reinterpret and reframe in inspirational modern terms the patriarchal assumptions of the letter to the Ephesians. There seems to be a great deal of potential in the epistle's quasi-mystical understanding of married sexual union.

> Husbands must love their wives as they love their own bodies; for a man to love his wife is for him to love himself. A man never hates his own body, but he feeds it and looks after it; and that is the way Christ treats the Church, because we are parts of his Body. This is why a man leaves his father and mother and becomes attached to his wife, and the two become one flesh. This mystery has great significance but I am applying it to Christ and the Church. (Eph 5:28-32)

Aspects of this would also be applicable to deeply intimate but not genital friendships between people whose sexuality is mature. *Eros*-love does transcend purely physical desire but it does not bypass it. When directed towards another human being, *eros*-love includes the physical but is not oriented *primarily or exclusively* to pleasure or to the release of physical tension. *Eros*-love strives ultimately for union with whatever we perceive to be the source of all value for us. Or, as the eminent American psychologist Rollo May suggested, *eros* is "the drive towards union with what we belong to." That is, towards harmony and unity and integrity and meaning. In Christian terms, this is not some impersonal force but is God-in-me, God-in-the-other, and God-as-the-love-between-us. This move towards union involves a process of transcending our sense of fragmentation and separation. In an alienated or dysfunctional culture, *eros*-love may actually be in conflict with the prevailing misshapen attitudes to "sex." A true *eros*-love views "the other," our partner, as a subject with whom we seek to be united rather than an object to be used for pleasure, release, or breeding.

There is an important difference between false eroticism and true *eros*-love. The first is an uncontrolled desire to draw other people into ourselves. It therefore tends to be invasive and possessive. Ultimately, if we are prone to false eroticism, we want to be gratified. We do not truly want other people for themselves. In contrast, *eros*-love is a unitive power bringing together elements that really belong to each other. The crucial thing is that desire is not purely instinctual. In terms of human sexual encounter, true desire is always a desire for another person mediated through his or her body and the experience of being joined with it. Spiritually, the human body is the sacrament of a person. A true erotic desire recognises the sacrament for what it is—something that points beyond itself to a profound unity between persons.

Augustine is the theologian most credited with establishing the central Christian attitudes to sex. It is sadly true that Augustine identified sinful concupiscence with sexual desire, which he interpreted as tainted at its very roots. Despite that, he did understand rightly that *eros*-love is at the heart of the search for God. "Our hearts are restless, Lord, until they find their repose in you" (*Confessions*, 12). Augustine knew that desire was not something we could or should uproot but was an essential mark of our humanity and our belonging to God. Rather, he suggested that the objects of desire or of *eros* need to be ordered in accordance with their true relationship to God. The erotic is well-ordered if it is radically open to the transcendent. Whatever criticisms may sometimes be laid at Augustine's door, this aspect of his thought has great merit.

In our experiences of sexual desire, love is not primarily universal even if it is ultimately open to universality. Sexual desire is particular, passionate, and embodied. In the same way, God, incarnate in the man Jesus, is revealed as passionately engaged with the particular circumstances of our world and with all people in particular. Sexual desire, if it runs deep, is similarly self-giving and committed. Yet the idea that the body language of human love is a concrete articulation of the love of God revealed in Jesus Christ seems pretty daring to some people. How can we compare the love of God with the urgent, painful, and sometimes wounding experiences of human longing and passion? And so, it has been commonplace to separate sex from the incarnation. Is it not the case that many people think that Jesus was like us in all things but . . . sex? But through the incarnation, God refuses to be seen as a proposition or abstraction. Instead, God becomes human in a physical, and therefore sexual, person who experienced pleasure, pain, and need.

The scandal is not in linking sex to Jesus or to God's self-giving but in the fact that our Christian faith, while based on a particular instance of embodied love, has so little place for the religious significance of the erotic. Theological discussion has usually been limited to sexual ethics—how an essentially physical reality can find outlets in safely prescribed contexts. If you think this statement is exaggerated, I invite you to ask yourself how many people you know, including yourself, would tell their spiritual history in terms based partly on sexual experience. How many of us, too, would see our sexual growth (pain or passion) as intimately associated with our following of Christ or as liberating us to enter more deeply into the desire of God?

We all need to move beyond our tendency to underestimate the erotic and reduce it to the fulfilment of social needs. Sexuality is about more than cementing stable families and reproducing the human race. It is this kind of reductionism, at least as much as a fear of bodily powers, that led sexual renunciation rather than sexual experience to become *the* way of spiritual growth and, therefore, the privileged icon of God's self-gift in Jesus. Spiritual elites "reproduced" through attracting recruits rather than through sexual interaction! As a result, sexual union became the province of the "secular," if not the profane, rather than of truly spiritual people. It is only in more recent times that a committed sexual relationship was capable of being understood as vocational.

If we go back to the story of the origins of Christian asceticism, to the Desert Fathers and Mothers of Syria, Palestine,
and Egypt, we will see that sexual temptation in itself was
often treated in a rather matter of fact way. Sexual desire was
seen, at least implicitly, especially in terms of a sharp antithe-
sis between the "world" and the "desert." To flee the world
was not so much to flee sex or the body. But it did involve
leaving a precise set of social relationships and constraints—
for example, the drive towards marriage, child-rearing, and
conscription into the settled land and its culture. The ideal
of living "like the angels" who do not marry (assumed to be
the lot of resurrected human beings as well) did not really
originate in a concern for physical purity, however it may
have been interpreted later. The assumed life of the angels
had more to do with a conception of perfected human society
which, it was thought, would be voluntary and harmonious
rather than based on purely conventional structures.

The above reference to the ultimate state of resurrected
people reminds us that where an overbalanced emphasis on
the afterlife has appeared in religious thinking, the inevitable
result is a devaluation of the erotic. It is perhaps not surprising
that the Hebrew Scriptures, which have a less well-developed
belief in bodily survival after death, are happier to emphasise the positive qualities in the present life of the erotic in
relation to the sacred. This raises important questions for us
as contemporary Christians. Can we experience, even if only
partially, what is of absolute value in the here and now? Are
we capable of reading spiritual depth into the enjoyment of
all good things as God's blessings and God's playfulness? Or
is *real* fulfilment and joy only to be found in the hereafter—a
better life in a better place? If the latter is the case, we will
tend to sacrifice what is seen as dubious pleasure now for
perfect joy later.

Intimacy

Here we are, you and I, and I hope a third, Christ is in
our midst.

God is friendship. . . . But still what is true of charity,
I surely do not hesitate to grant to friendship, since "he
that abides in friendship, abides in God, and God in him."
(Aelred of Rievaulx, *Spiritual Friendship*, 1.1, 69 and 70)

These words of Aelred, a twelfth-century English Cistercian, in his wonderful book on friendship, remind us that,
once again, it is important not to reduce our understanding
of sexuality to genital activity, as if this one area provides the
total meaning of love and intimacy. Sexuality in its broadest
sense covers our whole experience of embodiment. In other
words, our sexuality embraces a huge area of feelings and
emotions that move us towards other people. And this is true
of every kind of relationship, including those of single people.
Sexuality is, if you like, what enables all of us to express emotions such as tenderness, closeness, and compassion as well as
our general openness to touch.

"Intimacy" is a good word for expressing the side of our
sexuality that is involved in all our close relationships. It
follows that intimacy is not reserved to those people who
are thought of, in conventional terms, as "sexually active."
Each and every one of us is called to intimacy of some kind
with other human beings—with our parents and other family members as well as with close friends. Our problem is
that we tend to limit the idea of what "intimacy" means. In
general terms, all of us need to learn how to be intimate, in
appropriate and unthreatening ways, with people who are
not sexual partners.

The call to intimacy that all of us experience at different points in our lives is an invitation to take risks. For all
human love can come to an end, may deceive, is partial, and

is never totally and finally reliable. Yet our capacity and need for intimacy is a call to find *within* this risky human loving, the love of God that is total, constant, and faithful. Deep human friendship is a powerful contribution, arguably the most powerful, to a loving union with God. The call to intimacy also involves a realisation that however much two people love each other, they will never possess or own each other, nor will they ever fully know each other. There is always an area of inalienable strangeness in the other person. There is, therefore, forever the possibility of greater depth, of "more," in all relationships.

Whether we are single or in a committed, exclusive relationship of some kind, the Christian insights about *eros*-love and *agape*-love remind us that to become complete, we are all called to seek the eventual integration of particular and universal love. Only within our experiences of intimacy with other people, whether genital or not, may we learn a way of being fully present both to ourselves and to others rather than being superficial and remote in our emotional lives. The risk of intimacy, rather than the apparent security of emotional detachment, reveals the truth of ourselves, teaches us about availability, and educates us in truthful self-disclosure; of all human experiences it is the one most likely to provoke real change in us.

Another thing that the search for love reveals is the need for a balance between solitude and intimacy. What we find in our human relationships we will also find in our relationship with God. To say that solitude and intimacy need to remain in balance is to affirm two things. First, we need a sufficient degree of healthy rootedness in ourselves before we can move outwards to others in a non-abusive way. An Indian friend once commented, in the context of Western "spiritual seekers" wandering around India, that only those people who know where they come from and where they belong are safe to travel. This comment could just as well be applied to the journey of love as to geographical travel. "Solitude" describes that necessary place and time of waiting where we learn how to receive—ourselves, God, and other people—in disinterested love. The ability to receive in such a self-transcending way does not come easily. To learn to wait and then to learn the fruitful communication of intimacy is always painful, for it involves a stripping away of unreal expectations and selfish demands and yet, at the same time, a deepening and sharpening of true desire.

Second, an intimacy that is spiritually healthy always allows other people to remain securely in their own space. The German poet Rainer Rilke, in *Letters to a Young Poet*, suggested that real love does not consist in "merging" but means "that two solitudes protect and border and salute each other" (Rilke 1954, p. 59). That seems a wonderful description not only of human intimacy but also of God's intimacy with us revealed in and through human loving.

Liberation from Private Will

If we turn our thoughts again to the desert ascetics of the early centuries, we can see that they understood so well the greatest human emotional battle: how to overcome our divided hearts. In concrete terms this is the struggle in daily experience to be liberated from false and destructive individualism—the tyranny of private will. Paradoxically, the early Christians thought of sexual abstinence as important mainly as a symbol of a much wider struggle. They knew that the conflicts we all experience with the "desires of the flesh" reveal the more deeply rooted, essential flaws of the heart. These may be summarised in terms of self-centredness, self-seeking, and self-gratification of all kinds. The early ascetics sensed an absolute quality in the choice of sexual abstinence that made it a powerful symbol of the boundary between the spiritual innocence they desired and complicity with things of this world. The early ascetics were considered to be heroes not so much because they had risen totally above the needs of the flesh (which was never the case anyway) but because their bodily discipline gained them hearts that were all of a piece.

Today, these same desert values, which can be summed up as the desire for singleness of heart, are increasingly being rediscovered as the ideal at the centre of intimacy and sexual union. Many Christians are also convinced that the wider world needs to hear a new word about sexuality and its potential spiritual depths to counteract the superficiality of much media presentation. There is, however, a growing realisation that traditional Christian spirituality, unlike Judaism or Islam at their best, has generally failed to provide any explicit underpinning for the spiritual quality of sexuality. We need a new dimension to our Christian tradition in order to create the possibility of a deeper life in God within rather than outside a fully human sexual life.

When we allow ourselves to become aware of our sexual desire, we gain important indicators of the deeper and more complex levels of our existence. This awareness offers the possibility of growing into maturity not only psychologically but also spiritually. For example, our experience of sexual arousal tends to be seen as primarily an instinctual and physical force. It is, however, also a matter of personal power and as such is an opportunity for choice and discernment. This becomes an important context for opting into a way of existence based on values. In other words, we may be frequently aroused but we make choices as to whether to act on those feelings or not. Cultivating awareness of what comes into play as we are aroused, and as we choose to act or not act, is a deepening experience. Gradually, we learn to respond to arousal not with compulsive behaviour but by making choices based on self-awareness and the awareness of other people. This, in the best sense, is the moral dimension of sex. It is essentially linked to our inner life in the Spirit rather than simply to abstract rules and external authority. As we learn what we desire (both what we enjoy *and* what we need in the broadest sense) and learn to communicate it, we come to live increasingly in relation to it rather than to compulsion on the one hand or moral guilt on the other. This is the process of becoming a sexually mature person.

Sexuality is the testing ground of the integration or fragmentation of our personalities. I do not want to ignore the reality of sexual pathologies by appearing to retreat into a false and superficial lyricism in an idealised description of human love and sex. The very power of sex makes it impossible for it to be a neutral reality. Wrongly directed sex (as well as the sexual expression of our wrong directions) tends to be compulsive and destructive. Without doubt sex can bind us and make us incapable of fulfilling our responsibilities to ourselves and to others. It can also be insatiable, preventing us from ever feeling fulfilled. This is likely either to make us bitter with our partner who has "failed" us or angry about our apparent inability to find satisfactory partners at all. But my essential point here is that conflicted sexuality and misplaced sexual behaviour are indicators of much broader problems of maturity, freedom, and spiritual health.

The converse is true of a joyful and balanced sexual awareness, self-acceptance, and self-communication—and indeed self-transcendence—in which we find our greatest pleasure in the pleasure of the other. Equality, mutuality, and reciprocity are the hallmarks of a mature, free, non-possessive, non-abusive love. The depths of intimacy, including sexual union, are profoundly kenotic or self-giving in their direction. We are moved towards a shedding of our false selves and come to live and act more and more from within the truth of who we are. We grow in our capacity to be available, to be appropriately disclosed, to be strong yet vulnerable, deeply moved to change rather than to stand stubbornly and fearfully in the safe and known.

To give and to receive sexually has a sacramental quality as long as it truly aspires to be a gift of *self* and a joyful receiving of another person rather than merely an exchange of bodily stimulation. Spirit touches spirit. To borrow the old language about sacraments, "It is an outward sign of inward grace," of a deeper inner reality. Appropriate sexual body language is a sacrament of "real presence"—both the true and un-ashamed presence of one person to another and, within that and cementing that self-disclosure, the Real Presence of the incarnate, indwelling God. "This is my body—my life—given for you." "And they recognised him in the breaking of the bread." And we may recognise God, too, in the breaking open of bodies, the breaking open of self, for each other.

Sexual union is eucharistic, a liturgy that may heal and restore loving partners to a spiritual centredness. In this lit-urgy, union is capable of performing something with a deep meaning. Those who freely unite themselves to another come to know themselves at the same time as profoundly self-pos-sessed, rather than invaded or stolen. Here, desire becomes more than a physical urge and is discovered to be that power within us that enables us to overcome our fears of absorption. The acceptance of my body by another and my acceptance of theirs, in intimate touch and mutual delight, is ultimately transformed into a deepening sense of the wholesomeness of my *person*. As we truly come into possession of our self and learn to dwell in the self, we are also led into a movement beyond self to the other. And as, in turn, we come truly to dwell in the particular and personal love of another person we are lead even further by that same movement of open-ness. This does not occur without pain and struggle. But through deep intimacy we move slowly towards the horizon of non-exclusive, universal love where, as in God, *eros* and *agape* are found ultimately to be one.

Sexual Union and Union with God

There is a beautiful account of spiritual communion in
sexual intimacy in the extraordinary diary for the years 1941
to 1943, *An Interrupted Life*, composed by the young Dutch
Jew, Etty Hillesum.

> Perhaps that is the only real way of kissing a man. Not
> just out of sensuality but also from a desire to breathe
> for one moment through a single mouth. So that a
> single breath passes through both.
>
> And then for a short hour we had shared one breath as
> I had been wanting to do for many, many weeks. And I
> had rested so confidently and with so much surrender
> in his arms and yet full of sensual tension. But above
> everything else there was that shared breath. And in
> that short hour so much strength flowed into me that I
> believed I could live on it my whole life long. (Hillesum
> 1985, p. 117)

A number of people whom I know have found those words
to be a powerful expression of their own experiences, at least
at moments, of their intimate relations.

In the context of my own gradual awakening to the spiritual power of sexuality, one of the spiritual books that had
the greatest effect when I first read it in the mid-1970s was
the profound and beautifully written *Yes to God* by the late
Alan Ecclestone. Amongst other things, it daringly (or so I
thought at the time) had a chapter on "Spirituality and Sexual
Love." Perhaps that simple fact was for me, in the long term,
more important than the content of Ecclestone's words but
a number of his phrases and images remain with me. First,
sexuality represents our passion to become engaged. Second,
it is "a great hunger," "a perception of beauty," and "an intense pleasure." Yes, all of those things, but ordered in such
a way that "it challenges those divided by it to seek and find

at another level a unity of being." Most powerfully of all, Ecclestone concluded that,

> The primitive impulse to deify sexual love was not wholly misguided; it has all the features of great mystical experience, abandon, ecstasy, polarity, dying, rebirth and perfect union. . . . It prompts between human beings those features characteristic of prayer; a noticing, a paying attention, a form of address, a yearning to communicate at ever deeper levels of being, an attempt to reach a certain communion with the other. (Ecclestone 1975, p. 88)

If much mystical literature had traditionally used the language of sexual union to describe our relationship with God, Ecclestone turned this on its head. He used the language and experience of mysticism and prayer to express with great power the fullest potential of sexual union.

When sexual union is the consummation of deep, exclusive, and faithful love between two people, it may be a sacrament of that union with God, and in God with all that is, for which God has created and redeemed us. Shared sexual joy, as a step towards God rather than as a substitute for it, is a genuine act of worship, a genuine prayer. Etty Hillesum learned a great deal about this from her close friend and lover Julius Spier.

> To him everything is of a piece, he does not separate the physical from the spiritual and feels so close and familiar to me precisely because his life is so much more coherent than mine. (Hillesum 1985, p. 111)

Of course, there are other kinds of human communion and communication that have something of the same possibility, but the sexual union between faithful lovers involves an intensity, an abandonment, and yes, even an ecstasy, that makes this potentially the most powerful of symbols.

In his unusual attempt to reintegrate sexuality with religious mysticism (*The Meaning of Love*), the controversial

Russian theologian Vladimir Solovyev pointed out that the so-called higher animals paid less attention to pure multiplication of the species than the "lower" ones. Solovyev suggested that what he called "sex love" figured more strongly wherever the feeling of love for a unique person took on an unconditional importance—unconditional, not least, as to their capacity to be a good procreator! The desirability of the other is not dependent on her or his "usefulness" (Solovyov, 1945).

The ecstatic, even mystical, reading of sexual union has historically found more acceptance in parts of the Jewish tradition than in Christianity. In some quarters, the Song of Songs, while still associated with Passover time because it was taken to reflect the mutual love between God and the people of Israel, was also granted an explicitly interpersonal interpretation. Thus, it was sometimes read on the Sabbath evening as a reminder that the beginning of the Sabbath saw the arrival of a "Bride" who was to be welcomed. Sexual intercourse between spouses was also encouraged on the Sabbath night. To make love out of the fullness, relaxation, and joy of Sabbath was the earthly counterpart of the holy union that occurred on the Sabbath evening between the *shechinah* (the indwelling presence of God, sometimes seen as the feminine aspect) and the masculine aspect of God.

To draw a parallel between sexual expression and mystical union with God—as some Jewish traditions, Solovyev, and Ecclestone do—should not appear blasphemous for Christians. If there is a blasphemy it lies, rather, in the fact that sexual expression has been so downgraded that we find the parallel disconcerting. The intensity of union with a partner is no longer naturally associated with our calling in Christ to be drawn into the life of God, or what the Eastern Christian tradition calls "deification." Nor does union suggest the possibility of a participation by loving partners in the ecstatic, creative outpouring of God. This is far more than simply being procreators in a narrow, biological, child-bearing

sense. To have such a "high" view of participation in creation naturally has its painful side. Apparent "failures," such
as miscarriages or an inability to have children, are always
psychologically painful. There is, however, in addition, a *spiritual* pain involved when a couple's sexual relations include an
intense sense of participating in God's creative action.

It seems to me that the contemporary criticism of traditional
patriarchy in the West opens up the possibility of arriving at
a more positive evaluation of sex and of its conscious rein-
tegration into the sacred. A patriarchal way of seeing things
tends to give sacred significance mainly to the biological aspects of heterosexual sex. Thus, particular emphasis has been
placed, at least implicitly, on the active male fertilisation of
passive matter provided by a female incubator. The mystical-
sacred dimension of sexual union is effectively diminished in
such an unequal and non-inclusive understanding of sexuality. Instead of stepping back in awe at the mystery of sex, we
have also tended to prescribe how it should be conducted
and thus to atomise it. This diminishment of sex is true both
of pornography (sex is only for pleasure) and of a great deal
of Christian moral teaching (sex is only to make babies).
When compared to a richer vision, both views are revealed as
reductionist and functional, sometimes to a neurotic degree.

A Crossing of Boundaries

Various writers have suggested that sex and death are in-
terrelated, biologically, psychologically, and spiritually. This
makes a great deal of sense. For the religious person both
death and sex are channels of union with God and/or another
person that involve the dissolution of the boundaries that
normally identify us as individuals, distinct from other people
and all that surrounds us. The dissolution of boundaries can
take place without loss of personal identity. In this way, both
death and sex share in the traditional characteristics of mysti-

cism. Without doubt, to step beyond the familiar boundaries is always a risky business. Perhaps this is why death, sex, and mysticism have been viewed with equal fear and suspicion at times within the Christian community!

For adults, sexual relations may at times be a major source of ecstatic experiences. We have been conditioned, however, not to think of them in this way. For this would be to encroach on the domain of the sacred that traditionally was presumed to lie beyond such profane things as sex. There has also been a tendency in Christian mystical theory to limit the "ecstatic" to a very narrow band of extraordinary experiences that are given to very few people. Fortunately, there is a contrary movement today, accepted—albeit with caution—even by more conservative religious writers, to understand "mysticism" as a much more widespread and everyday reality than has traditionally been appreciated. If this is so, then sexual union has the potential to be one of the primary God-given channels in human life for such experience.

Whether interpreted broadly or more narrowly, ecstasy may best be understood precisely as an experience of the temporary dissolution of the normal boundaries of perception and living. The Jewish diarist Etty Hillesum at times experienced intimacy in a similar way.

> He leant against the wall of Dicky's room and I leant gently and lightly against him, just as I had done on countless similar occasions in the past, but this time it suddenly felt as if the sky had fallen as in a Greek tragedy. For a moment my senses were totally confused and I felt as though I was standing with him in the centre of infinite space—pervaded by threats but also filled with eternity. In that moment a great change took place within us, for ever. (Hillesum 1985, pp. 172–73)

Ecstasy is a moment in which some otherwise distant reality is glimpsed as here and now and at one with oneself. This is a peak experience. Whether in the context of contemplation or sexual relations, it is something that it is dangerous and damaging to grasp for its own sake. It is, after all, possible to become addicted to altered states of consciousness, whether produced by drugs, by sex, or even by meditative practice. But such addiction is to mistake the means for the end. Peak experiences have their place in any fully human life and are *not* to be viewed with suspicion. But in contemplative mysticism, the particular experiences exist in order to transform the whole of life. So, the ecstasy of sexual union, and the temporary dissolution of boundaries involved with it, serve the more general transformation of two people and their growing together into union on every level of their being. In other words, the unitive "glimpses" that sexual or contemplative ecstasy provides serve to deepen our personalities and to deepen our perceptions of the way reality is.

Sexual ecstasy, while involving some form of bodily self-giving, is more than bodily in the sense that it concerns the blending together of two people. In other words, it is profoundly associated with intimacy. Intimacy with another human being (of which bodily self-giving is a powerful but not exclusive symbol) is the privileged context for experiencing the immanence of God.

We need to maintain a certain delicacy here. Just as with God's relationship with us, in the same way human intimacy involves holding in proper balance an appropriate dissolution of personal boundaries and yet continued respect for personal space. It is an unfortunate fact, of which we are made increasingly aware every day, that the sexual crossing of boundaries has often been violent and abusive. At the heart of most cases of sexual abuse, including rape, lies the desire to gain power over another human being. Sexual violation of boundaries is used to meet a number of needs that have nothing to do with healthy sexual desire, let alone with true love.

True human desire, just like God's desire for us, is respectfully attuned both to the self and to the partner. Each person may be lost in the other, but individual boundaries are not abused or invaded. Each person freely allows them to be crossed in a way that enhances each partner rather than destroys either person's identity.

Chapter Five

Desire and Choosing

To reach satisfaction in all
desire its possession in nothing.
To come to possess all
desire the possession of nothing.
To arrive at being all
desire to be nothing.
To come to the knowledge of all
desire the knowledge of nothing.
To come to the pleasure you have not
you must go by a way in which you enjoy not.
To come to the knowledge you have not
you must go by a way in which you know not.
To come to the possession you have not
you must go by a way in which you possess not.
To come to be what you are not
you must go by a way in which you are not.

—John of the Cross, *The Ascent of Mount Carmel*,
bk. 1, chap. 13, v. 11

Whether we are familiar with the original language of John of the Cross or more used to the paraphrase by T. S. Eliot in his poem "East Coker," the way to spiritual perfection presented in the quotation above could be interpreted as one of unremitting and unattractive negativity. The journey suggested by John of the Cross, however, is one of desire. And desire, with its connotation of incompleteness, is more importantly an image of movement and change. From childhood onwards, we all have to learn that to grow up involves leaving the familiar and the controllable, to travel through places and experiences that are not familiar. These are where "you are not."

Yet, paradoxically, it is also in this journey through the loss of childhood certainties and securities that we come more and more to a firm sense of our own identity and to the ability to make autonomous choices. In the process of maturing, we hopefully move, whether consciously or not, from fulfilling the expectations and desires of others to a greater realisation of our own desires and the appropriateness of choosing for ourselves. If we are unwilling to leave the security of what is known, we will never arrive anywhere. "To reach satisfaction in all, desire its possession in nothing." If we cannot let go of trying to accumulate many different things, we will never discover what having "all" means.

To Live Is to Choose

To be truly alive, not least because it is to grow and to change, is continually to make choices. There is a sense in which we come to be as persons through our many experiences of choosing. It is a paradox that we can only move towards what John of the Cross calls "satisfaction in all" by making choices. For to choose also, and always, means to abandon something, to let go of certain things, to exclude other courses of action. "To reach satisfaction in all, desire its possession in . . . *no thing*." The explanation is that our movement towards embracing "the all," the truly inclusive, is not the same as our attempts to accumulate more and more different objects or particular people in our lives. "Satisfaction in all" in the sense implied by John of the Cross is not a matter of seeking to fill our emptiness with an increase of possessions.

Ignatius Loyola has a different kind of spirituality from John of the Cross. Yet, in his teaching on discernment, he understood something of the same dynamic when he wrote in his *Spiritual Exercises* of the need always to desire "the more," and for "indifference" or "detachment." It is possible to understand the words in rather negative terms. Understood properly, however, "indifference" and "detachment" are really extremely positive because they are concerned with reaching an ever greater degree of inner freedom. Such freedom cannot be artificially constructed. It is a gift of God's grace. Yet it is what is needed in order to grow inwardly from the level of immediate wants to that of our deepest desire. There is a journey into the cave of the heart where our essential self and God both dwell. The problem is that we are often the prisoners of our immediate and urgent neediness. Our way of accumulating possessions can be a desperate sign of our fear of being nothing, or becoming nothing. It is all too easy to mistake the temporary assuaging of our needs for "satisfaction in all."

So choosing (or discerning how to choose) does not simply involve detached, rational thinking, even though there has to be a place for that. We have, in a sense, to dive headlong into our experience, into our desires, in order to discern truly. Aristotle's notion of "practical wisdom," which influenced Christian thinking on discernment, is rooted in emotional engagement and desire. It grows not by stepping back from experience but through our immersion in the everyday. For to discern our deepest desire involves an act of commitment as well as an experience of enlightenment. To discern is not, on the one hand, purely a deeper level of awareness or, on the other, merely a decision. It ultimately involves moving further towards a harmonious relationship with who we most genuinely are as people. This, in turn, means coming to a realistic acceptance of how we are situated in the world of place and events. Discernment, in other words, is a matter of continually reaching out for integrity.

The diary of Etty Hillesum, leading up to her departure for Auschwitz in 1943, records her painful yet joyful struggle to reach the greatest possible degree of spiritual integrity. Etty's whole diary is the record of a painful process of discernment and choice—increasingly from within her deepest self as well as from within the truth of her circumstances and relationships. In this unfolding self-awareness and self-acceptance, Etty also encountered God with an intensity that was perhaps mystical.

> I sometimes actually drop to my knees beside my bed, even on a cold winter night. And I listen in to myself, allow myself to be led, not by anything on the outside, but by what wells up from within. (Hillesum 1985, p. 81)

To discover the truth of our heart's desire is also to recognise something familiar, even if it is to know it explicitly for the first time. It is in some sense, therefore, a return to the sources of our being. Our desires have the capacity to reveal truth, for the latter is not ultimately some abstract reality to be reached by means of conceptual thinking alone. As the famous Thai Buddhist master Achaan Chaa suggests, "At some point your heart will tell itself what to do."

Realising Our Destiny

Without suggesting a fatalistic view of human life, this approach to choosing has a great deal to do with coming to understand and then grasping wholeheartedly our particular "destiny." Once we have understood our "destiny" for what it is there is a kind of inevitability about it, because it is so intimately associated with our identities as individual persons. It is not something imposed from outside by a God who acts like some puppet master of the universe who makes demands of us irrespective of our circumstances. On the contrary, destiny is "what lies in us"; it is our special gift. This does not make it painless for, like Etty Hillesum in Nazi-occupied Holland, it may impel us to make courageous choices that even our closest friends cannot fully understand.

> And it is right to feel sick and confused and unsettled for once, like today, full of cold fear and uncertainty, and a sigh of "Good God, child, what are you letting yourself in for?" But also a growing sense of self-certainty. I have matured enough to assume my "destiny," to cease living an accidental life. . . . Now I have a right to a "destiny." It is no longer a romantic dream or the thirst for adventure, or for love, all of which can drive you to commit mad and irresponsible acts. No, it is a terrible, sacred, inner seriousness, difficult and at the same time inevitable. (Hillesum 1985, p. 138)

The spiritual journey mapped out in their distinctive ways by John of the Cross and Ignatius Loyola demands courage, *cor agere*, to act from the heart. We act from the heart by being attuned to the truth of our desires. To reach that kind of attunement is not a simple matter. There is ultimately no method by which we can learn how to discern effectively and infallibly on every occasion. The key to discernment is not technique but the focused intensity of our desire. It is a matter of attitude and of relationships—the quality of how we relate to our own self, to other people, to created reality, and to God. Etty Hillesum talked of a mysterious inner regulator growing within her.

> I still believe I have an inner regulator, which warns me every time I take the wrong path by bringing on a "depression." If only I remain honest and open with myself and determined enough to become what I must be and to do what my conscience commands, then everything will turn out all right. (Hillesum 1985, p. 203)

Having said this, it is possible to place ourselves more in a position where this quality of relatedness may be deepened.

Meditation in all its forms ultimately seeks to cultivate attentiveness and awareness. Both of these are vital ingredients of a discerning heart. Yet, sometimes it takes considerable patience and trust to believe in this kind of meditative "doing nothing." The contemporary American writer Ken Wilber, in a book about his wife Treya and her spiritual journey, quotes her as saying:

> When I wonder why I sit . . . I say to myself that I sit to express myself as I am at this moment. . . . Perhaps later purpose will come clear. . . . [P]erhaps purpose is already here, unfolding as I go. (Wilber 1991, p. 162)

Sometimes the birth of converted attitudes and of deepened ways of relating has to take place in darkness, in patient waiting. Light somehow needs the darkness in order to be known. Without embracing the darkness, we miss the light. Darkness and waiting sharpen desire, test its depths, and lead us to a point where we simply have to let go. We find so often that meaning lies in the very waiting. Sadly, for most of us, waiting is extremely difficult in a consumer culture where immediate satisfaction, and simple methods of achieving it, are presented as of overwhelming importance.

From Many Desires to Deepest Desire

Because discernment is a journey, we will find ourselves moving, slowly perhaps, from an initial awareness of a multitude of desires, wants, and needs (and probably a relatively undiscriminating search for their satisfaction) to the deeper levels of our self. It may also be seen as a movement from awareness of desire to responsible action in the light of that awareness. It is important, however, to remember that the other levels of desire we encounter and pass through on the way are not irrelevant. We will never come to know our deepest desire except through attention to the many desires. If we think of our experience in terms of a circle, we stand on the rim, the circumference, where we are in contact with a plurality of feelings, experiences, and needs. Not so much in a harmonious, inclusive way as in a confusing one. "I have so many desires, I don't know what to do with them." But it is in fearless engagement with this confusion, rather than simply by some activity of our rational, detached intellect, that we move towards our centre. The many desires are necessary staging posts on a journey towards what is most true in us. Ignatius Loyola, in his *Spiritual Exercises* (no. 23), expressed something of this idea when he suggested that we should relate to created things "to the extent that they help us towards our end."

The scriptural story of the Samaritan woman at the well in the Gospel of John, chapter 4, provides us with a striking image of the relationship between our initial needs and our deep desires. The woman is led by the conversation with Jesus from an immediate sense of needing fresh water to her deeper desire for "the spring of water within, welling up for eternal life." Even through the pain of being confronted with her many failures in human relationships, the Samaritan woman approaches a more truthful sense of her identity and of the power of God that is being made available to her. The woman also learned from Jesus in the context of confronting her history of relationships that to attend to desires, and to discern between them, is a process of becoming more passionately focused on what is life-giving rather than destructive. This, once again, is what the author of *The Cloud of Unknowing* implies by our need to stand in "naked intent," and what Ignatius Loyola means by suggesting in his *Spiritual Exercises* that we should ask for what we desire at the beginning of prayer.

Different Kinds of Desire?

When we think about the discernment of our desires, it is important to remember that each of us is a single, unified human being, even if we all have many dimensions. The problem is that so often in practice we tend to distinguish between the emotional, intellectual, physical, and spiritual parts of ourselves. And so we divide up our "passions" according to their association with one particular aspect of our human existence. Yet, these dimensions of our personality, and the kinds of desires associated with them, exist in a continuous interdependence. Thus, the way we treat our bodies affects the deepest longings of our spirits. And our spiritual desires find their expression in our immediate feelings and in our bodily reactions. Over many years, I have slowly learned, thanks to spiritual directors and friends, to pay more attention to the way that changes in my body are indicators of spiritual well-being or spiritual confusion. It is important to grasp that our so-called spiritual desires do not exist in a separate compartment of life. The whole of life is spiritual. We cannot say that any desire is irrelevant to the process of spiritual growth and discernment. Every kind of desire is touched by the Spirit of God in some sense, even if it is capable of being misdirected.

One of the most common, and also most difficult, human experiences is that of being pulled in opposite directions by apparently contradictory desires. This is particularly true when these desires, in the first instant, seem good and important. We find ourselves powerfully, almost willy-nilly, drawn towards people, objects, and ideals that are not merely diverse but sometimes incompatible. We are sometimes moved by passions that fragment us, perhaps violently so. In this context, discernment is the way of sifting through a confusion of desires so that our lives can be shaped by the best of them. The "best of them" does not imply that we live in a two-tier universe in which certain types of human desires are inherently better or that "the best" are immediately recognisable. We are all the products, and sometimes the victims, of our upbringing and environment. Sometimes we have to struggle against assuming that we must always make certain kinds of choices if we are to be "good Christians."

Great Desires

For each of us, however, in our own distinctive way, certain desires have the potential to shape our most serious choices and therefore give direction to our lives. These are what Ignatius Loyola called "great desires." Active commitment to a great cause would fall into that category—for example, to be with Christ and to play a part, with others, in establishing the kingdom of God throughout the world. The self-giving of everyday disinterested love—or the desire for it—would be another. At the other end of the spectrum, some desires speak of instant needs or immediate satisfaction in matters that are petty rather than life-directional. Or worse, as we saw in the introduction, some desires can be perverted.

It is, of course, only too easy to mistake the desire for personal satisfaction for the answer to life's mystery—but that is what the art of discernment is all about. As a process, discernment enables us, in the first instance, to be aware of and to accept the full range of desires that we experience. From this starting point, we are slowly led to understand the way in which our desires vary greatly in their quality. Certain desires, or ways of desiring, if we follow them through, will tend to push towards a dispersion of our spiritual and psychic energy or a fragmentation of our attention, experience, and personalities. Other desires seem, rather, to promise a greater concentration of energy and a harmonious centredness. What is sometimes initially confusing is that the less helpful or healthy desires appear to be more strikingly attractive because they make us feel good. In other words, the direction and potential of our desires is not always immediately self-evident. To come to appreciate these things demands patient reflection.

Desire and Ignatian Discernment

Reflection on our feeling experiences, with a view to choosing the greater good, is the central feature of the Christian tradition of discernment. Apart from the Scriptures, this wisdom tradition was shaped by ancient philosophy. For example, the Greek philosopher Aristotle, in his *Nichomachaean Ethics*, suggested that good choices should be made by reflecting on our sense of ultimate purpose. This "practical wisdom," however, demands attention to our feelings, including "desire," as we immerse ourselves in the everyday. For Aristotle, we can shape desire to achieve balance or "moderation," which is also an important aspect of discernment in early monastic writers such as John Cassian. Aristotle suggests intentionally engaging in appropriate actions in response to situations (related to a true sense of purpose), even if we do not feel inclined. This closely resembles Ignatius Loyola's notion of *agere contra* in his *Spiritual Exercises*—consciously acting against self-serving instincts.

Overall, Ignatius's *Spiritual Exercises* offer one of the most effective summaries of the discernment tradition. Perhaps the most helpful element of his teaching is the importance he gives to our ability to identify two basic kinds of affective experience, which he calls consolation and desolation, and to act appropriately in relation to each (nos. 313–336). This is not just a matter of undertaking intense introspection in order to uncover all our possible motivations, even if the beginning of discernment consists of recognising various desires within our heart and psyche.

When we reflect on desires as the basis for making choices, we can spend a lot of time trying to work out where such desires come from or what inspires them. This is not always very easy. In fact, for Ignatius, it is much less helpful to search for the roots of our actions than to focus on the direction in which our desires and longings are moving and the deeper moods that they create. Discernment is all about recognising the energies that drive us. What kind of energy is being released? As someone once said to me, Ignatius recognised that we can experience two kinds of "buzz" and that their immediate intensity is not the most reliable indicator of their ultimate truthfulness. So, when Ignatius Loyola wrote about "inner movements," he was not simply referring to the depth of disturbance or the strength of feelings. He was suggesting that all desires and feelings have a direction. Some desires are life-giving and others are ultimately destructive.

The basic characteristics of what Ignatius Loyola means by consolation are: an increase of love of God as well as a deepening of human love, an increase of hope and faith, an interior joy, an attraction towards the spiritual, a deep tranquillity, and peace. It is vitally important to remember that Ignatius is not talking about the immediately pleasurable. There exists something that might be called "tough" consolation. This involves a healthy realisation of our own brokenness as well as a sharpened sensitivity to the pain of the world. There is often a paradox in consolation. "Interior joy," or "deep peace," produced by a realisation of the power, love, and faithfulness of God, can go hand in hand with a great deal of external disturbance and pain.

Perhaps one of the most striking experiences I have ever had of what this kind of consolation means came during the extended period which went on for several years when I was struggling with whether to remain in religious life. I was staying at a remote monastery in New Mexico as part of a reading and writing sabbatical and was not consciously focussing on life decisions at the time. One day I was sitting under a tree by the river that ran by the monastery quietly waiting for the bell to ring for Vespers. Without any warning or process of conscious decision-making, I was suddenly aware that I would leave the Order, although there was no sense of time scale. It was a moment of immediacy and utter clarity that presented me with a certainty that could not be contradicted. The experience was so powerful that I can visualise the moment and the place quite vividly all these years later. In one way I sensed that this expressed an inner truth. At the same time, however, the experience also felt that it came from beyond myself. Underlying this experience was a deep peace about the truth of the situation that never left me, even though I struggled for a year or so more with a great deal of pain and sadness and with my reluctance to face up to change.

In contrast to consolation, desolation may initially feel quite pleasant and attractive. Whether on the surface or deep down, however, desolation ultimately reveals itself as drawing us in destructive directions. Ignatius suggests that its key characteristics are the opposite of how he describes consolation. So there is a decrease of faith or hope or the capacity to love truly. There is turmoil and confusion at a deep level rather than merely surface disturbance. There is a tendency towards impulsive behavior, especially in the direction of emotional or physical self-indulgence. Other feelings that Ignatius lists include listlessness, tepidity, unhappiness, and a sense of separation from God. It is too simple, however, to say that desolation is the same as the experience of depression or "feeling bad." Psychological depression and spiritual desolation may overlap at times, but they are not the same thing. There are people who suffer from lifelong clinical depression who may, nonetheless, be said to be in consolation because they never quite lose touch with the love and faithfulness of God as their deepest truth.

Throughout his *Spiritual Exercises*, Ignatius Loyola returns again and again to the subject of desire, which is always directed towards deeper and more healthy ways of choosing.

For Ignatius, the spiritual journey is essentially away from fragmentation and towards harmony, from the surface to the centre, from spiritual imprisonment towards inner freedom. The whole point of our "spiritual activities" is to be gradually rid of what he calls "disordered affections" (no. 1). This movement away from disordered feelings and needs that tend to entrap us is what Ignatius means by the somewhat unattractive word "indifference" (no. 23). This is not a cold absence of feeling or a dispassionate detachment. "Indifference" involves reaching out towards our deepest desire, which is to be what we were created for. Once we have recognised the disorder in our inclinations, it is possible to help the process of freedom along by consciously seeking to focus our attention, as well as our actions, on the opposite (no. 16).

It is clear, however, that Ignatius Loyola does not see the answer to discernment and spiritual growth in terms essentially of human effort and will power. On the contrary, while we may prepare ourselves and open ourselves, it is God who alone puts proper order into our desires. Ignatius also recognised wisely that we cannot honestly desire to take a life-enhancing direction overnight. So he suggested that we may be capable only of desiring to have the desire! And that spark, that chink in our defensive armour, is all that God needs. Positively, if we engage with our desires on this journey towards spiritual freedom, it means moving from a mainly intellectual perception of God towards an inner "savouring" of God's reality in the depths of our being (no. 2). It also demands that we enter into the journey with deep generosity and commitment (no. 5). Ignatius, however, warns us that this should not be confused with an intensity of fervour that might lead us to hasty responses (no. 14). Sometimes, as Mary did in the story of the annunciation in the Gospel of Luke, we need to check the credentials of our apparent inner experiences of God. Perhaps we need even to interrogate God before we act on what seem to be God's promptings or give our wholehearted commitment to them!

> But her whole body pulls away.
> Only her head, already haloed, bows,
> acquiescing. And though she will, she's not yet said,
> *Behold, I am the handmaid of the Lord,*
> as Botticelli, in his great pity,
> lets her refuse, accept, refuse, and think again.
> (Hudgins 1991, "The Cestello Annunciation")

Meditations of Desire

Two crucial meditations in the second phase, or what Ignatius Loyola calls the "Second Week," of the *Spiritual Exercises* seem to me to illustrate graphically different levels or qualities of desire. The Meditation on Three Classes of People (nos. 149–157) and the Meditation on Three Ways of Being Humble (nos. 165–168) are associated, in the process of the Exercises, with what Ignatius describes as making "an election." An election means choosing a way of life that is single-heartedly concerned with "the purpose for which I am created" (who I am) and with "desiring to serve God" (my sense of ultimate meaning).

In the Meditation on Three Classes of People, the different levels of desire are illustrated in reference to three people who have each received rather a lot of money. The first person recognises the need at a certain level to be free of unhealthy dependence on the money yet does nothing at all about it. The second person desires the same freedom but equally desires to retain the money—an attempt to balance two conflicting desires. The third person desires to be free but, interestingly, does not mind whether the money is kept or not. The desire for freedom is deep enough that it can cope with either having money or not having money.

In the other meditation, the first way of being humble describes the minimum level, or quality, of desire. This relates to a belief that we will be saved, and that it is sufficient in order to be saved, merely by being obedient to the law of God. This seems to speak both of a certain minimalism and of a spirituality of duty. The second way of being humble is described in terms of facing options that seem to be "equally effective for the service of God our Lord and the salvation of my soul." In this kind of humility, we do not desire overwhelmingly one way or another. So the second way is focused on freedom and what Ignatius calls "indifference." Interestingly, the third way of being humble, that moves beyond either duty or detachment, is described by Ignatius as "the most perfect." Here, our desire is simply to be like Christ, whatever that means in our particular circumstances. This is not so much by imitating precisely the actions of the human Jesus as recorded in Scripture. Essentially it points to reaching the deepest possible level of attunement to the reality of God in me. "May they all be one. Father may they be one in us, as you are in me and I am in you" (John 17:21).

The endpoint of the journey of discernment and choice, when we are in contact with our ultimate desire and live fully in tune with it, is summarised in the "Contemplation to Attain Love" at the end of the *Spiritual Exercises* (nos. 230–237). All through the process of the Exercises, Ignatius Loyola has asked the person undertaking them to focus intently during prayer on that level of desire that seems to be the key to the particular moment on the journey. This reaches a climax in the "Contemplation to Attain Love" as a desire for an all-embracing realisation of and response to God in all things.

> Here [what I desire] will be to ask for interior knowledge of all the great good I have received, in order that, stirred to profound gratitude, I may become able to love and serve the Divine Majesty in all things. (no. 233)

It would be unrealistic to suppose that any of us live at this level of spiritual realisation on a daily basis! But in the Contemplation, Ignatius offers a kind of mysticism of finding God in all things to which we can aspire and which we probably touch at moments.

Deepest Desires and God's Desiring

The process of discernment can be understood as a way of moving from the surface of our lives, the place of many desires, to our centre, our soul or our essential self, whatever we prefer to call it. Here, where we are in contact with our deepest desire, we find that we are essentially and simply attuned to God.

> There is a really deep well inside me. And in it dwells God.
>
> Sometimes I am there too. But more often stones and grit block the well, and God is buried beneath. Then He must be dug out again. (Hillesum 1985, p. 44)

As Etty Hillesum knew well, it would be a mistake to pretend that this journey to our centre proceeds along a simple straight line. At different moments we move in and out— sometimes nearer the surface of our lives, sometimes nearer the centre.

It is certain that none of us, not even people we call saints, move totally and finally beyond the more superficial or even less healthy desires. We are brought back to them, again and again. Sometimes this feels disconcerting and depressing. But in fact we never repeat things precisely in the same way. Human progress through life could be described as rather like a spiral. This continually curls back on itself and yet is always moving deeper.

Overall, if we pursue the spiritual journey honestly and attentively, we will be able to touch our centre more frequently and its power in our lives will be more consistently released. We know those moments of being in touch with our centre particularly when we have a deep well-being beyond immediate pleasures, gratifications, or satisfactions. The latter, on deeper reflection, merely cloak our sense of emptiness, pain, or darkness.

The journey of desire moves us beyond a sense of seeking to conform to an understanding of the "will of God" that is arbitrary and totally detached from our actual experience of living. Rather, we are drawn ever deeper into God's desiring within our lives and personalities. This is not static, predetermined, or extrinsic to the kind of persons we are. God's desiring in us is expressed in and through what we come to see as our deepest desires. True, this may initially be seen as in conflict with more immediately recognisable needs and wants, but God's desires in us do not conflict with our "best interests" or deepest self. The desire we seek to touch and to draw on has been described by spiritual writers variously as the "spark of God" in our soul, what God has implanted in us or the truth of our being. But can we always trust our experience of desires? We can if we befriend them and then test them rather than try to ignore them or bypass them. Only then can we gradually learn how to distinguish deep desire from wants and the "desires" that are motivated by fear from the desires that are genuinely part of a pattern of consolation.

In the end, there is no infallible *guarantee* that we will choose rightly as Ignatius Loyola reminds us in his comments on making an "election" or choice of a way of life.

> When that election or decision has been made, the person who has made it ought with great diligence to go to prayer before God our Lord and to offer him that election, that the Divine Majesty may be pleased to receive and confirm it, if it is conducive to his greater service and praise (no. 183).

Our process of choosing can only be handed over to God and the "rightness" of particular choices will be confirmed only in the long term—that is to say, within the totality of our life story. During the final period of my process of leaving religious life after so many years doubts inevitably arose about the correctness of the decision. I found that I was greatly supported by the words of a great hymn by Charles Wesley that we sang in chapel of the college where I worked at that time.

> Jesus, confirm my heart's desire
> To work, and speak, and think for Thee;
> Still let me guard the holy fire,
> And still stir up Thy gift in me.

A Contemplative Experience

There is a point at which any attempt to write about desire and discernment begins to run out of vocabulary! This is precisely because what we are considering is not a skill or method but a contemplative process that leads us towards the centre that we call God. Contemplation is not static, even though the great contemplative writers often speak of waiting or stillness, or being rather than doing, as metaphors for the experience. Despite some modern writers on the subject, contemplation is more than just an optional or freely chosen technique of prayer and meditation. It is an ever-deepening way of conversion, profound change and of purification by fire. In it, our desires are transformed, intensified, concentrated to the point where choice, commitment, and action inevitably follow.

Our difficulty with pinning down the whole business in words actually models the inconclusive feeling of the process of discernment and of seeking to make our choices from the standpoint of authentic desire rather than from an easily defined "objective" and disengaged position. To enter into our desires contemplatively is to enter into a way of mystery and darkness and therefore of loss of control and, ultimately, of abandonment to God.

There are several characteristics present in the experience of moving from "many desires" to "deepest desire" out of which we seek to make life choices. One important feature that people talk about is a deep and lasting contentment beyond transient pleasure. The place of deepest desire is one where we know that we are touching a deep well of peace and truthfulness that speaks of the infinite—even if we have passed through disturbance and pain on the way. It is also a place where we engage with what we ultimately realise is intimately associated with our identity. That is why choices made in this place are to do with life directions rather than with the relatively trivial. Our capacity for commitment is engaged. Modern advertisers, of course, realise all this and are experts at making us think that their products do not merely satisfy some surface want but are actually vital to our identity.

To be even momentarily in our centre, the place of deepest desire, is not necessarily an emotionally intense experience. Ultimately, however, it is recognised as an encounter with our own spirit and also with what we call God. Such experience is somehow so real that we cannot properly name it. Yet we cannot deny its validity and importance either. Equally, in its presence we are simply not able to remain unchanged with integrity or with a sense of peace. There is, in other words, a dimension of conversion involved. That is what marks out such experiences from insights arrived at and decisions made solely with the rational, objective mind.

This does not mean that these experiences of conversion do not need some testing. It is my experience, and that of many people in spiritual ministry, that increasing numbers of people seeking spiritual guidance have no extended religious background or nurture in a faith community. They are the products of adult conversion experiences, sometimes of a fairly dramatic kind, or are on some kind of spiritual quest. Quite a few of such people, in the initial intensity of a new-found desire for God, assume that a vocation to ministry or to some lifestyle that involves a radical change of direction is inevitably the consequence. Such a change seems to be a better expression of their total commitment. It is vital to help such people to reflect whether, and to what degree, such feelings are congruent with their whole personality and the rest of their life and experience. Often they are not.

A second characteristic of our deepest desire is that while it may be located metaphorically at the "centre" of our being, it is not self-centred. It involves a movement away from isolation and introspection towards harmony or union within ourselves, with God and with all people and things. True contemplation and the process of moving inwards to the depths of our desire do not isolate us from surrounding reality. It may help to return to my image of the circle. If our journey takes us to its centre, and if we live and choose from that centre, it becomes a point of unity, concentration, and connection rather than of exclusion. It is the hub, as it were, of all desiring. The many desires of our surface consciousness, that is, on the circumference of the circle, are not simply lost but discovered to be enveloped in a wholeness and inclusiveness which fulfils and completes them in an unexpected way.

A further characteristic of the search for our deepest desire is a movement from being imprisoned or overly enraptured by the multitude of apparently desirable things towards being free to choose authentically, clearly, and with integrity. There will be some point in life (or perhaps a number of points) when we come to know ourselves to be controlled or defined by so many things outside ourselves—misshapen images of God, an over-developed sense of duty, the expectations of other people. Then there is a gradual struggle towards liberation where we come not only to feel free to choose from the depths of our being but also where God is enabled to choose in and through each of us. As a friend once put it to me, this is an experience of really *choosing* rather than of "being chosen for."

To learn how to choose freely is also to learn a great deal about dying—about letting go of much that is apparently necessary, satisfying, and good in life in favour of what is ultimately better. Such deaths happen daily. In the resurrection narrative of the Gospel of John, Mary of Magdala seems to have been confronted with the hard lesson of being asked to let go of a certain kind of human and spiritual consolation—the familiar way that Jesus had been present to her up to that point. This was in order that Jesus' mission be fulfilled. Only then could a greater good prevail for her and for the other disciples. "Do not cling to me, because I have not yet ascended to the Father" (John 20:17).

But clinging to the familiar is a natural human reaction. Somehow it is only possible to move on when we know that what is offered to us has greater potential. Classical spirituality gave the impression that we had to become detached before we could respond to God's promptings. My experience, however, is that in practice, the order of events is different. We actually find ourselves being strongly attracted towards something better and *then* find that we have already begun to be freed from what held us back.

Conflicts and Blocks

Of course, it would be unrealistic to pretend that the process of seeking to live out of our deepest desire is problem free. There are clearly going to be moments when we feel a great deal of inner conflict. Is every desire I experience good in itself? Is every desire implanted in me by God? Is there ever such a thing as an evil desire? After all, the writer of Psalm 140 prays, "Do not grant the desires of the wicked, O Lord" (v. 8). These questions regularly arise in retreats and spiritual direction. They imply that there are situations where the relatively simple distinction between desires and surface satisfactions cannot easily be applied. To a great extent, these questions lie at the heart of what Ignatius Loyola teaches about the confusing spiritual experience of "temptation under the guise of good."

> It is characteristic of the evil angel, who takes on the appearance of an angel of light, to enter by going along the same way as the devout soul and then to exit by his own way with success for himself. That is, he brings good and holy thoughts attractive to such an upright soul and then strives little by little to get his own way, by enticing the soul over to his own hidden deceits and evil intentions. (no. 332)

Behind this rather dated language lies an important perception that even our best motives, our capacity for great commitments, can be perverted and channelled into directions that are ultimately destructive, just as our capacity for love can be abused.

One of the most painful experiences of all arises when we find that what seems to be genuinely our heart's desire is continually hindered with apparently insuperable obstacles. This inevitably raises the question of what this is actually saying about my deepest desire. Is what we are focusing on really our deepest desire, not in the sense of most passionately held, but in the sense of what is truly of ultimate concern to me? Are we perhaps associating a true desire with a specific way of living it out or enabling it to be realised? Are we actually choosing wholeheartedly and freely or, if the truth be known, are the obstacles that appear to be outside me or brought about by "circumstances beyond our control" still within us? The external world of events that affect us and the internal world of our own motivations and attitudes have an uncanny way of relating closely to each other.

It would be unfair to pretend that these questions always solve the dilemma. Sometimes, therefore, we may have to face the mystery of "the right time" for things to happen. I have certainly had the feeling myself, and frequently hear other people say, "Why didn't I do that earlier? Why couldn't I bring myself to make that decision? Why couldn't I see that twenty years ago? Why has so much time been wasted?" But the reality is that we may have to wait until all kinds of inner and outer factors are in appropriate relationship. Sometimes we really can do no more than sit with the desire and the obstacles and wait for the meaning.

Hearkening unto Myself

Ultimately, the truth of discernment and choosing lies in a patient "reposing in oneself," as Etty Hillesum put it in her diary. "And that part of myself, that deepest and richest part in which I repose, is what I call 'God.'" The work of the spirit is to "hearken unto" self, others, and God.

> Truly, my life is one long hearkening unto my self and unto others, unto God. And if I say that I hearken, it is really God who hearkens inside me. The most essential and deepest in me hearkening unto the most essential and deepest in the other. God to God. (Hillesum 1985, p. 214)

Chapter Six

Desire and Change

Because you are not there
When I turn, but are in the turning,
Gloria . . .

. . . destinations are the familiarities
from which the traveller must set out . . .

. . . What matter
if we should never arrive
to breed or to winter
in the climate of our conception?

Enough we have been given wings
and a needle in the mind
to respond to his bleak north. . . .

—R. S. Thomas, *Mass for Hard Times*

Human desire can be interpreted as a permanent openness to what is other than ourselves and to what is beyond our boundaries. Desire is precisely a sense of incompleteness and, therefore, it becomes the condition of our openness to possibility, to future, and to the "always more," the infinite. God always calls to us from out of our future and comes to us from our future. There is in desire something about our living in a permanently liminal state.

As body-spirit people, we naturally bridge two worlds—the world of here and now material reality and the "other" world that we have traditionally called the world of the spirit. Celtic Christianity, which had such a vibrant role in Britain and Ireland in the early Middle Ages, placed great importance on edges and boundaries of all kinds. These were often associated with particular geographical locations or natural features. The religious settlements of hermits or monastics sometimes gathered there. There were places with specific associations, such as a cemetery which was so obviously a "passing through" place. There was, of course, above all, the sea, which for the Celtic wanderers or "pilgrims for Christ" was not simply a route somewhere but an archetypal symbol of a deliberate spiritual displacement. It was the massive and powerful "between place" that was never far away in Celtic islands. Here, wayfarers were, like the Israelites in the desert, always "on the way." It might be said that the sea was a place of desire as the pilgrims searched above all else for what they called "the place of their resurrection."

Fact of Change

Human life as a spiritual journey is a continuous process of change, a story of endings and new beginnings. Indeed, we have to come to terms with the fact that change is the norm in human life rather than the exception. The notion that stability, fixed points, being utterly certain, or possessing all we need is what we should expect is questionable. Rather, movement, change, and a lack of definitive clarity are what we live with most of the time. The other moments are occasional resting places. There is, therefore, an immense difference between linking spirituality purely *to* our experience of changes, important though that is, and creating a spirituality *of* change that would enable us to live within a condition of permanent transition.

The theme of death and rebirth is a recurrent one in our lives. Our experiences of loss, and even pointlessness, may later lead to a sense of new life gradually taking shape. But we cannot escape prematurely from the passages of life in themselves. Indeed, our bodies insist that we take seriously the rhythms of change. For example, puberty and adolescence are inescapable. There is also no choice, ultimately, in the natural process of aging, however much we nowadays seek to hide it.

All loss is frightening, especially when it means the loss of much that has been previously valued and enjoyed. Our experience of change may be long drawn out and even agonizing. The problem is that none of us seem to be very good at radical change! We are better at clinging to the safe and known while perhaps adjusting ourselves a little—a kind of psychological swaying with the wind. We so often get caught up in the miseries and confusions of what we are losing. As a result, we find that we are unwilling to believe that new life is anything more than a distant promise. It is important for all of us to discover that the power of the resurrection made available to us is not something deferred but instead is already present now as the key to all that is happening to us and around us.

Commenting some years ago on a spate of conversions to the Roman Catholic Church by a number of prominent Anglicans, a friend remarked that it was the desire for "a backdrop of certainty." My reaction was that even if this were true, it should not be! It is a fact, however, that so many of us have been brought up to expect certainty in our religious lives, or at least to think of it as the ideal. The poet T. S. Eliot seems to have held, with Aristotle, that perfection lies in being "at rest" or still rather than in movement. Consequently, he felt ambivalent about desire as the last few lines of his poem "Burnt Norton" show:

> Desire itself is movement
> not in itself desirable;
> Love is itself unmoving,

only the cause and end of movement, timeless and
    undesiring,
except in the aspect of time
caught in the form of limitation
between unbeing and being.

It seems to me that a belief in absolute human certainty conflicts with the reality of desire for the infinite that is inherently part of our human condition. Desire involves openness to movement, to the fact that there is always "more" beyond our vision and grasp, to a continual potential for change. From the point of view of our present experience, the sense that we can achieve absolute certainty once and for all is a dangerous illusion.

Clearly part of our human instincts finds the experience of uncertainty profoundly disturbing. Maybe it is to compensate for this that we tend to create a vision of life after death, specifically of heaven, as a condition that will provide us with all that we feel we lack in the present life. This form of projection of our fears means that an afterlife is traditionally thought of as *contrasting* in all respects with our life now rather than *completing* or fulfilling it. We lose any sense of there being a profound continuity with our essential human experience in the present. An excessively therapeutic mentality in Western culture spends a great deal of time trying to deny death as much as possible. Yet because it cannot be avoided, the hope seems to be that there will be a final healing beyond death of all our ills—particularly change, movement, and that very uncertainty of which death is the continual reminder.

Stages of Transition

The fact of continual change does not mean that there are no specific experiences of transition to be gone through. We cannot dictate in advance how long those experiences of transition will last. Nor can we dictate how transition will occur for each of us or on every possible occasion. We need to grow in patience and really learn to trust our experiences for what they are. There is also a right moment for particular stages of transition to come to completion. For example, we may know that it is healthy for children to leave home and we may grow anxious about whether we are holding them back. Yet, there is also a danger in being artificially doctrinaire about the timing of it all.

Even though transitions and changes are very subjective experiences for each of us, it is possible to make some general remarks and then to map out some of the more common stages. Transition marks a boundary between two situations of *relative* stability—"relative" because in reality there are no situations of complete stability and lack of movement in human life. At some level of our life and experience, there is continual change and development. Our body cells change, are replaced, and die all the time. In all transitions there is a movement or passage from a particular set of circumstances to another. As in the parable of seed growing by itself, however, the movement may be both hidden and prolonged.

> [Jesus] also said, "This is what the kingdom of God is like. A man throws seed on the land. Night and day, while he sleeps, when he is awake, the seed is sprouting and growing; how he does not know. Of its own accord the land produces first the shoot, then the ear, then the full grain in the ear. And when the crop is ready, he loses no time: he starts to reap because the harvest has come." (Mark 4:26-29)

The transition or boundary place is where, as far as our consciousness is concerned, we can only wait. Because a process of personal change involves a shift from one life structure to another, there is obviously both a departure and an arrival. The experience of waiting is sometimes a purging of our need for the securities of the past and a place where the intensity of our desire for growth is increased. The final departure, or letting go of what is past, has to take its time. The arrival at what is new, and the complete focus of our energies on it, cannot be complete until the ending of the previous life structure is complete. Sometimes this final ending extends over time even while we live predominantly in the new. Perhaps for many of us the incompleteness of our transitions is something we have to live with.

There are, as I said, a number of broad stages that seem to be common to our experiences of change and transition. Initially, the realisation of a profound transition can simply immobilise us. We are struck dumb as the familiar landmarks and our normal strategies of control slip out of our grasp. Then there may be a kind of regrouping of our forces as we convince ourselves that the transition is either not happening at all or is not really all that significant. Either way, we will tend to minimise what is happening to us or pretend that what appears to be our experience is not really true. The predominant feeling is relief but it is likely to be short-lived because it is artificial.

Next we are likely to sink into depression and fear as we realise that we are being challenged more profoundly than we had hitherto anticipated. At this stage, there is a real stripping of illusions that we have to go through. Sometimes that takes us pretty deep into the darkness. It is likely to be there, in an example of paradoxical consolation, that we come to an acceptance of our present situation as "real." There then follows an important experience of letting go—at least to a degree that is sufficient to move us onwards beyond the darkness. On the way forward, we will naturally need to test out what the new reality is and how we should respond in practical terms. Our previously accepted framework of meaning and structures of commitment will have been undermined in the transition, and so we will need to spend time searching for what should replace them. Finally, if we continue on a healthy path, the whole experience will be internalised and will become the reality out of which we live in a committed way.

That description is a broad overview of experiences of transition. It certainly fits pretty well with the painful process of transition in my own life when, after years in a religious community, I sought to leave. Someone once pointed out to me that this description also fits our experiences of failure and coming to terms with them. But then, it seems to me, moments of failure are a type of transition as we are invited to move from protecting the self we prefer to project to an acceptance of the real self.

We do need to be cautious, however. First, life is rarely quite as neat as our attempts to provide an overview of it! We should not fool ourselves, for example, that our lives move in straight lines or in well-ordered, successive stages where one experience or growth point can be said to be complete once and for all. Second, this way of describing transition can make it sound purely psychological. On a certain level it is. Change, however, also has a spiritual dimension which, while not absolutely distinguishable from other levels of our lives, intimately touches our sense of identity before God. It even affects our perception and acceptance of God's own identity.

The spiritual dimension of letting go and of major transitions has sometimes been described in the Christian tradition in terms of a "dark night." Here there is real spiritual pain that engages the level of faith as well as the level of the psyche. John of the Cross, in *The Dark Night*, suggests that there is first of all a "night of sense" in which a person learns to let go of familiar externals—even spiritual ones like forms of prayer or long-standing lifestyles. Then there is a "night of the spirit," or dark night of the soul, in which we are stripped of all spiritual gratification or tangible consolation. Only then will the dawn of a new reality finally break through.

Change and Commitment

A spirituality that takes desire seriously as one of its driving forces and recognises that change is a permanent part of the equation necessarily needs a sense of provisionality. Ultimate truth or fulfilment is never to be found in any specific *this* or *that*, whether a time, a place, or a person. But a spirituality of provisionality does not contradict the ability, or indeed the need, to make commitments. Our desire is always searching for something within which to become consciously grounded—in other words, a sense of commitment.

All true commitments include risk and exclude total certainty. Anyone who has made any kind of solemn commitment or promise in private or public, including marriage or religious vows, knows this only too well. Without this balance of risk and provisionality, we could not make the commitments in the first place. Nor could we make sense spiritually of the ending of relationships, or the way people leave particular contexts of commitment after many years. Difficult, too, to make sense even of the fact that there are natural endings within human commitments—for example when our children leave home or our partner dies. Provisionality enables us to make sense of faithfulness and continuity (our own and God's) within the risk of commitment and, at the same time, in these experiences of painful change.

In reality, we can only discern the truth of our desires and the focus of our commitments at any given moment as best we can—that is, provisionally. At some point, we need to stop prevaricating and choose to risk a commitment. Even though I spent my childhood close to the sea, I still tend to hesitate before diving into water of any kind. I fear the shock of the cold. But in the end, I cannot decide what the water might be like to swim in simply by sitting on the rocks and wondering! The problem with commitment is that it is not static or fully realised in the moment of first decision. Commitment is itself a journey.

We are right if we think that human commitments are dangerous, because unpredictable, and if we hesitate at the prospect. Perhaps, we sometimes think, it would be kinder to ourselves and to others not to enter such uncertain territory. This is particularly true if we have been taught that commitment depends on our own willpower and effort, and that once we have made a visible commitment, we have an absolute duty to remain faithful to all its surrounding circumstances. "You've made your bed, so lie on it!" The catch is that if we try to defend ourselves with all kinds of qualifying clauses in our heads before we undertake any commitment, it ends up being no commitment at all.

It helps to be able to know that it is a mysterious God at the heart of our mysterious selves that forms the level of deepest commitment to which our desires draw us and to which we need to remain faithful if we are to remain whole. In the process of leaving the religious community I had belonged to for many years, I had to face the issue of faithfulness head on. It's an emotional business. If I left community, what sense could I make of the commitment I had made? What would faithfulness mean then? The question of faithfulness covered both my relationship with God and my relationship with a particular group of people. Then there was the struggle to believe in God's faithfulness to me in the midst of all of this. It helped me immensely when I was helped to understand the difference between the deepest level of commitment and the contexts of life where we try to work these commitments out. These contexts are not only necessary but also are all that we have in life. Slowly it became possible to accept that even within a framework of my deepest commitment, it could be valid to move elsewhere. Indeed, I was gradually enabled to think in terms of actually being led elsewhere rather than merely indulging a personal fancy. Our commitments always need to be properly grounded and embodied in specific contexts or relationships, but it would be false to pretend that any human context is absolute in itself.

The experiences of commitment and choice, therefore, have two dimensions. First, we need to be wholeheartedly engaged. But second, in terms of the human contexts within which we express our commitments, we need to see that they are always a risk and are always, therefore, in some sense provisional.

Like love itself, the experience of being drawn towards our deepest desire, and having it unfold before us, can be testing, stressful, and rather like sailing in uncharted seas. It is hard to remain true to this sense of being called, of being drawn into a mysterious and deeper truth when it involves, as it often does, shedding the security of many familiar landmarks and assumptions. The most profound test of our trust in God, as well as of our own resolve, occurs when this sense of call initially appears to confuse the people we love and respect, to contradict some of our long-standing loyalties and ties, and to appear "irrational." The directions set by love and the search for an inner integrity frequently do not correspond to the canons of "the sensible."

Conversion

As we noted briefly in the introduction, inner struggle is part of everyone's spiritual journey and takes many forms. The traditional monastic vow of *conversatio morum*, "conversion of manners," speaks of a commitment to permanent change and therefore of vulnerability. In so far as our baptismal call is to live within the power of the resurrection, this vulnerability is entirely appropriate. An important icon of risen life is that Jesus is present to his disciples with open wounds. Woundedness retains its depth even if transfigured and glorified.

Although we think of monasticism primarily in terms of stability, a desire for and commitment to change as a condition of living is also central to the Rule of St Benedict. The early Desert Fathers and Mothers recommended to their disciples, "Stay in your cell and it will teach you everything." Clearly it is important not to run away from where our struggles are based. That is what stability implies. Yet, at the same time, we are always people who must desire to move on. This *conversatio*, conversion, implies a radical response on our part to Jesus' words, "Come, follow me." We need stability, but we also need to live provisionally and to travel light.

The call to change also means that we and our desires are continually confronted with the challenge to be converted and to choose between reality and unreality. Just as change is a process not a moment, so conversion is an unfolding state of mind and heart rather than a static or self-contained moment. The God who is at the heart of change and to whom we are converted ultimately eludes us. There is always a new aspect. Whatever illumination we receive, we are always left at a new "square one." There is, however, a consistent temptation to turn aside from the search for a true vision of God and to settle for one aspect, one face of God, and to call it "all." We try to capture the fullness of God in one moment and then to hold on to the moment.

The danger of so-called conversion experiences, particularly in our Western consumer culture, is that the language we use can give the impression that a task has been fully accomplished. Spiritually, we will now live happily ever after. We have arrived at a condition of rest that is human perfection. But in fact, the reality is not like this, and everything is not under control. Conversion is more likely to mean that things, perhaps for the first time in our lives, get out of control. To be transfigured like Jesus we need to die spiritually. But real dying involves losing the illusion of control. That is why it is such a struggle. Conversion is always to another state of provisionality rather than a simple movement from chaos and uncertainty to the rock of final invulnerability.

The goal of the spiritual journey, God, is ever-expanding as far as our perceptions are concerned. The experience is not a commodity called "perfection" but a process of being continually filled. It involves responsiveness rather than grasping. For this, we have to give up the search for the horizons we find humanly so necessary—especially tangible progress and visible success. Conversion leads us to respond only to the "coordinates of grace" rather than to expectations, our own or other people's.

So, conversion is a time of chaos, searching, and the loss of paradigms. Yet it is, at the same time, a period of choice and of creativity. In its spiritual dimension, true conversion involves both grieving and celebration. As with all change in general, there is a turning away from something and a turning to a new direction. Too often the popular language of conversion experiences sounds as if all conversion is from sin to grace, from bad things to good things. This is too black and white, and it also gives the impression that conversion is essentially only a moral question. As an elderly priest I once knew said in a powerful homily, "I have found that the hardest thing is not to choose between good and bad but between what is good and what is better."

Without entering into the complexities of theological debate about the nature of conversion, there seem to me to be a number of things that may be said about it in relation to desire and change. First, conversion is not purely intellectual (a change of mind), nor is it purely moral (a change of behaviour). From the religious perspective, conversion has a certain emotional quality to it because it is tied up with our desire for God and for ultimate spiritual completion as persons. There is also a profundity to conversion that moves it beyond a merely routine shift of behaviour, an increase of knowledge, or decision to join some new institution or group of people.

The profound changes that can validly be described in terms of conversion engage our commitment, ultimately of every dimension of ourselves, head, heart, psyche, and spirit. While we may have difficulty in speaking of Jesus being "converted" in a moral sense, it is certainly possible to speak of the "conversion" of Jesus in a broader sense. Jesus undoubtedly had to face a crisis of meaning and identity in his life and responded to it by rethinking his relationship to God, his Father. There are two key texts here, which follow on from each other in the narratives of the Synoptic Gospels: Jesus' baptism in the Jordan and his temptations in the wilderness (Matt 3:13–4:11; Mark 1:9-13; Luke 3:21-22; 4:1-13). The whole sequence acts, as it were, as a process of conversion. In the unconditional acceptance of Jesus by God in the baptism, there was a true call. This is followed by Jesus' acceptance of his mission and a reordering of his priorities of which the temptations story provides a powerful symbol. The wilderness narratives in particular offer a classic expression of the free surrender of a sense of absolute autonomy as well as of a denial of those self-serving desires that interfere with a single-minded commitment to God in love.

In later Christian tradition, many people single out Augustine's *Confessions* as the classic conversion text. Although a turning from sin (*metanoia* or repentance) is involved, this is not the whole story. Nor is Augustine's account simply of a philosophical conversion in the sense of some conclusion to a search for intellectual truth. Augustine's conversion was an experience of inner transformation that had a great deal to do with desire. Indeed, it may be seen as the transformation of Augustine's desire from being directed at self-satisfaction to a powerfully focused yearning for God.

In a sense, the conversion of both the human Jesus and of Augustine centre around love and desire. Both the human Jesus and Augustine sought and struggled with the call to love without limits. In both human loving and our love of God, the conversion process is one of decentring, that is, of moving beyond seeing the self as the unquestioned centre of reality.

The deep change that is involved in conversion is a radical surrender but a surrender in *love*. Only falling in love, both with another person and with God, makes it really possible for us to surrender the self to any significant degree at all.

Desire and Journey

The experience of conversion and the process of change has been particularly symbolised in the Jewish and Christian traditions by "wilderness" in its various forms. There was the desert of the Israelites and the early Christian hermits or the sea of the Celtic wanderers. In contrast (and partly unfairly without doubt), the temptation to settle too readily and too fully has been symbolised by the city.

There is a tension in the Hebrew tradition between a sense, on the one hand, that the desert wanderings recounted in the Exodus narrative were the time and place of a true encounter with God and, on the other, the sense that God and God's promise was powerfully present in the particular place of the Chosen Land. In the desert there was no abiding city, merely a God who continually called the people onwards to new places of encounter, which could only be reached by faithfulness to God alone. Yet the land is a central theme of biblical faith. This land of promise was *the* sign of the covenant between God and the people. Eventually Sion, Jerusalem, and especially the temple became associated in a special way with God's presence.

So, two theologies existed side by side in the Hebrew Scriptures, sometimes uncomfortably so. The theology of the "Moses" school of thinking was always sharply aware of the spiritual temptations of settling down and becoming too fixed in our ways. The experience of wandering, of desiring but never totally arriving, of complete trust in God, was central. The contrasting theology of the "King David" school reflected the experience of coming into possession of the land, of settlement and of developing a temple cult. The desert was an ambiguous symbol of trial and tribulation that did eventually come to an end in the fulfilment of God's promise to bring the descendants of Abraham into possession of the land.

The founding Scriptures of Christianity are deeply embedded in the Jewish experience of defeat, exile, and ceasing to be a nation that was inextricably linked to a special sacred landscape. Much of the writing of the New Testament was born in the Jewish diaspora. This gave early Christianity a context in which spiritually, as well as physically, it moved out from its roots in the life of Jesus and the early disciples in rural Palestine. Eventually it became a faith that expanded through missionary journeying throughout the breadth of the Roman Empire. The theology is of a people on the move. Christians are "people of the way." The most characteristic lifestyle of the recorded heroes is the journey. The whole of this present life was considered to be pretty fragile, a liminal moment prior to the final dramatic arrival of God's kingdom.

One of the later Christian traditions that picked up this theme of movement and journey and turned it into a focus for spiritual desire was the Celtic, especially the Irish, one. "We stole away because we wanted for the love of God to be on pilgrimage, we cared not whither." In this way, according to the Anglo-Saxon Chronicle of 891, some Irish monks spoke to King Alfred after they had landed in Cornwall in a boat without a rudder. Wandering for the love of God caused astonishment and admiration. The development of *peregrinatio*, wandering exile, was one of the most extraordinary aspects of the spirituality of the islands of Britain, especially Ireland. For five hundred years Irish pilgrims left homeland, friends, security, certainties, and stability and set out for the unknown, desiring to be totally trusting in God.

In one of his sermons, St. Columbanus, one of the greatest of Irish wanderers, preached that all Christians are to be *hospites mundi*, "guests of the world."

> It is the end of the road that travellers look for and de-
> sire, and because we are travellers and pilgrims through
> this world, it is the road's end, that is of our lives, that
> we should always be thinking about.

The key was not just change, journeying, and movement
in themselves, but in them continually "to seek the place of
our resurrection." The outer journey was a powerful symbol
of the inner journey of deep desire to be in harmony with
the sacred—the same inner journey undertaken by the Celtic
solitaries who never left their homeland.

> Alone in my little oratory without a single human being
> in my company; dear to me would such a pilgrimage
> be before going to meet death. (Murphy 1956, no. 9)

To journey physically simply indicated an acceptance of
a permanent condition of change or transition in life and
in relation to everything around. It focused human desire
away from settling for a mere "this" or "that." By letting go
of all the things, places, and people that they held dear, the
Celtic wanderers sought to root out all desires that were for
less than all. The conditions of the Celtic ascetics may have
been extreme and their behaviour very radical if not positively
foolhardy, but the wanderers remind us in a romantic and
dramatic way of the inner journey of desire that all Christians,
and indeed all humans, are called to undertake.

Desire and Eternity

Are the experiences we have in this world of uncertainty,
change, and journeying meant inevitably to lead our desire in
the direction of an eternity of changeless certainty? Or, on the
contrary, have we missed the point if we think the present is
disconnected from, and merely the waiting room for, a future
"real" life? Is it, perhaps, that the continually changing quality

of our present life does not so much point to the next world as a kind of compensation as suggest our need to be purged now of a misleading desire for a final moment of completion and full possession of God?

This has a great deal to do with our image of God and of our essential self in relation to God. Is God beyond time, eternally the same and immune from change of any kind? In a world of flux and change, do we not need the stability of God? Is that what heaven and being with God means for us as well? I am not at all sure that our affirmation of relationships within God (Trinity) and God's engagement with us in love (creation and incarnation) make it possible to eliminate all notion of change from God. The dynamic quality of God-as-Trinity, who is being-in-relationship, points to a dynamic rather than static view of eternity. Change and response rather than changelessness expresses the being of God whose nature is to be vulnerable in love. The God who is at the heart of change always ultimately eludes us.

> He is such a fast God,
> always before us and
> leaving as we arrive.
> (Thomas 1984, "Pilgrimages")

There is always a new aspect to this God. For every definition we arrive at and every spiritual experience we think of as definitive or life-changing merely becomes another square one. We always have to begin the journey again with God although, equally, we are always tempted to turn aside from the vision that feeds our insatiable desire and to settle for one seemingly comforting aspect of God. We try to capture the moment and turn it into a commodity.

To live with the true God will eternally be an experience of non-possession, the provisionality of all our perceptions, and will always contain an element of unknowing in that our affirmation of God will never be complete or *be* God. We need to talk of perpetual change in our knowledge of God and to say that desire will always be a force that is integral to our relationship with God.

I am not sure that death promises us the end of time in every sense. What is spoken of by the Christian tradition is the end of *temporality*. This does not strike me as the same thing at all. *Temporality* implies loss, decay, and the passing away of things. *Eternity*, whatever it might mean, does not seem to imply sheer timelessness, even if it may involve transcending, in some kind of simultaneous vision, the limitations of our experience of time as merely a succession of utterly distinct moments.

Yet, for Augustine, when desire achieves its goal in heaven, perfect knowledge follows. For heavenly knowledge and desire are of the same reality: God who is love. True wisdom, tasted but not fulfilled in this material life, is "the knowledge and love of him who always is, and never changes, namely God" ('Homily on Psalm 135.8'). All in all, Augustine's understanding of desire and knowledge seems to add up to the notion that the enjoyment of heaven will totally satisfy our desire to know and to love. This static understanding of eternal life, however, is balanced by other texts. Interestingly, Augustine asks whether, if we are to love God eternally, we will also be eternally seeking God. His response is that just as our love for a friend who is close at hand in this life grows, so our love of God in heaven will always grow. "As love grows, the search for the one who has been found also increases" ('Homily on Psalm 104.3').

What drives the whole process of existence for a human being is the desire for God, that is, *eros*. This implies a perpetual and not accidental process of growth and change. Love is always dynamic because never completed. It is always incomplete because it is forever open to new "revelation" about the one who is loved. Love is always open to new things because at no point does it possess the other. With God especially, we can never talk about grasping or finally naming God. There is a paradox in Augustine's notion that our hearts ultimately find *rest* in God. If it is rest, it is not because our heart's desire is dimmed.

The early Eastern theologian Gregory of Nyssa also seems to argue that our desire for God inherently involves a perpetual movement.

> Certainly whoever pursues true virtue participates in nothing other than God, because he is himself absolute virtue. Since, then, those who know what is good by nature desire participation in it, and since this good has no limit, the participant's desire itself necessarily has no stopping place but stretches out with the limitless. (*Life of Moses*, bk. 1.7)

> Every desire for the Good which is attracted to that ascent constantly expands as one progresses in pressing on to the Good. (bk. 2.238)

> This truly is the vision of God: never to be satisfied in the desire to see him. But one must always, by looking at what he can see, rekindle his desire to see more. Thus, no limit would interrupt growth in the ascent to God, since no limit to the Good can be found nor is the increasing of desire for the Good brought to an end because it is satisfied. (bk. 2.239)

For Gregory, perfection lies in a continual movement onwards rather than in some static completion. Equally, while there may be a "true" vision of God, it is nevertheless the case that all possible visions of God are deficient in relation to what God fully is. So God appears to Gregory to say "the place with me is so great that the one running in it is never able to cease from his progress" (bk. 2.242).

What we speak of as heaven, or being with God for all eternity, is the final goal of what writers such as Gregory of Nyssa understood by the mystical ascent to God that was the

call of every Christian as the result of baptism. In the powerful words of the French thinker, the late Michel de Certeau,
mystical experience is to be caught up in "an eternity without
shores." Because God has no shoreline, as it were, the desiring
of our hearts will also, I believe, prove to be of infinite extent
and duration.

> He or she is a mystic who cannot stop walking and, with
> the certainty of what is lacking, knows of every place
> and object that it is *not that*; one cannot stay *there* nor
> be content with *that*. Desire creates an excess. Places
> are exceeded, passed, lost behind it. It makes one go
> further, elsewhere. It lives nowhere. (De Certeau 1992,
> p. 299)

References

Aelred of Rievaulx. *Spiritual Friendship*. Kalamazoo, MI: Cistercian Publications, 1977.

Augustine. *Confessions*. There are several modern editions available.

Bonaventure. *The Soul's Journey into God*. New York: Paulist Press, 1978.

Catherine of Siena. *The Dialogue*. New York: Paulist Press, 1980.

The Cloud of Unknowing. New York: Paulist Press, 1981.

De Certeau, Michel. *The Mystic Fable*. Chicago: University of Chicago Press, 1992.

Dillard, Annie. *Pilgrim at Tinker Creek*. New York: HarperCollins, 1977.

Donne, John. *Poetical Works*. Oxford: Oxford University Press, 1971.

Ecclestone, Alan. *Yes to God*. London: Darton, Longman & Todd, 1975.

Eckhart, Meister. *Teacher and Preacher*. New York: Paulist Press, 1986.

———. *The Essential Sermons, Commentaries, Treatises and Defense*. New York: Paulist Press, 1981.

Eliot, T. S. *Collected Poems*. New York: Harcourt Brace, 1963.

Gethin, Rupert. *The Foundations of Buddhism*. Oxford: Oxford University Press, 1998.

Gregory of Nyssa. *The Life of Moses*. New York: Paulist Press, 1978.

Hadewijch. *The Complete Works*. New York: Paulist Press, 1981.

Hill, Susan. *Air and Angels*. London: Mandarin, 1992.

Hillesum, Etty. *An Interrupted Life*. New York: Washington Square Press, 1985.

Hudgins, Andrew. *The Never-Ending*. Boston: Houghton Mifflin, 1991.

Hughes, Gerard J. *Aristotle on Ethics*. London/New York: Routledge, 2001.

Ignatius of Loyola. *Spiritual Exercises & Selected Works*. New York: Paulist Press, 1991.

John of the Cross. *Selected Writings*. New York: Paulist Press, 1987.

Julian of Norwich. *Showings*. New York: Paulist Press, 1978.

Lamott, Anne. *Traveling Mercies*. New York: Doubleday, 2000.

Murphy, Gerard. *Early Irish Lyrics*. Oxford: Oxford University Press, 1956.

Pseudo-Dionysius. *The Complete Works*. New York: Paulist Press, 1987.

Rilke, Rainer Maria. *Letters to a Young Poet*. New York: Norton, 1954.

Sheldrake, Philip. *Heaven in Ordinary: George Herbert and His Writings*. Norwich: Canterbury Press, 2009.

Slater, Ann Pasternak, ed. *George Herbert: The Complete English Works*. London: "Everyman's Library 204," David Campbell Publishers, 1995.

Sobrino, Jon. *Christology at the Crossroads*. Maryknoll, NY: Orbis Books, 1978.

Solovyov, Vladimir. *The Meaning of Love*. London: The Centenary Press, 1945.

Teresa of Avila. *The Interior Castle*. New York: Paulist Press, 1979.

———. *The Way of Perfection*. In *The Complete Works of St Teresa of Jesus*. Edited by E. Allison Peers. Vol. 2. New York: Sheed & Ward, 1950.

Thomas, R. S. *Mass for Hard Times*. Newcastle upon Tyne: Bloodaxe Books, 1992.

———. *Later Poems*. London: Macmillan, 1984.

Tillich, Paul. *Systematic Theology*. Vol. 3. Chicago: University of Chicago Press, 1963.

———. *New Being*. New York: Scribners, 1955.

———. *Love, Power & Justice*. New York: Oxford University Press, 1954.

Traherne, Thomas. *Selected Poems & Prose*. London/New York: Penguin Books, 1991.

———. *Centuries*. London: Mowbray, 1975.

Ward, Benedicta, ed. *The Sayings of the Desert Fathers*. Kalamazoo, MI: Cistercian Publications, 1984.

Wilber, Ken. *Grace and Grit: Spirituality and Healing in the Life and Death of Treya Killam Wilber*. Boston: Shambala, 1991.